Do words fascinate you? Do you wonder how words came about?

If you like learning about the origins of words and how new words develop, you will find this book offers hours of entertainment.

What's more, you will acquire a storehouse of knowledge in an easy, enjoyable way.

The book also provides many interesting quizzes that challenge your insight and imagination.

WORD DETECTIVE

Edward Horowitz, Ph.D.

HART PUBLISHING COMPANY, INC.
NEW YORK CITY

Contents

WORD
DETECTIVE

Man Learns to Speak— and to Write

How did language begin?

This is a very important question to which there is a very simple answer—we do not know.

Language began so long ago that it is virtually impossible for us to wrest the secret of its origin from the murky past. Primitive humans needed desperately to communicate with one another, to warn each other of danger, to express their common wants and passions; but in those ancient days, people did not speak. They cried in terror or pain; they smiled and frowned; they screamed and gestured. *But they had no words.*

And then—exactly how it happened we will never know—language was born. The first word uttered by man was a momentous act of invention.

Possibly, the first words were the names of animals, and were simply imitations of the sounds the animals made. A lion may have been called *rara*; a snake, *sss*; a bird, *tsip-tsip*. This childishly simple way of naming may have suggested to early man the idea of giving names to all the other things his eyes could see.

All we know for sure is that somehow the strange splendor of human speech developed. Of all living creatures, man alone has the precious gift of verbally expressing the thoughts that flow through his mind.

It is important to realize that language existed for thousands of years before writing was developed. People spoke about complicated ideas, and composed and handed down beautiful oral poetry with hundreds of verses, long before they could write a single syllable.

How did writing begin? There are three clearly defined stages in the development of writing:

The First Stage—Picture Writing

In the first stage of writing, people did the simplest and most natural thing of all: they made pictures of whatever it was they wanted to tell about. If a man wanted to report that his house burned down, he would draw a picture of a burning building. If a woman's arm was broken, she would draw a stick figure showing a broken arm.

Picture writing was universally the first step in written communication between people. Among the American Indians, picture writing was particularly highly developed. But picture writing had enormous disadvantages. People could write only about the most obvious physical things. They could not write about friendship, about love, or about any other abstraction. They couldn't possibly indicate in writing such concepts as "my son," or "my neighbor is a thief."

Not only was picture writing very clumsy, it was altogether inadequate to indicate the complex emotional and intellectual experiences of ancient man.

The Second Stage—Hierogylyphics

The second stage in writing, first developed among the ancient Egyptians, was a gigantic step forward. Using the pictures from their picture-writing system, the Egyptian scribes made each picture stand for a syllable whenever that syllable occurred in speech. These pictorial characters are called hieroglyphs.

Since you probably don't know Egyptian, we will use English words to illustrate hieroglyphics. Although the words are English, we will be doing exactly the same thing the Egyptian scribes did four thousand years ago. For example:

Initially in Egyptian picture-writing, the picture of a sun ☀ stood only for the heavenly body, the sun. Then the Egyptian scribes decided that the picture of the sun stood for the syllable *sun* anytime this syllable occurred in speech. Thus the picture of a sun would represent a *son* or the first half of the word *Sunday*.

The picture of a carpenter's tool, a saw, would signify the verb *saw*, as in *he saw*.

The picture of a bee and a leaf would stand for the concept *belief*.

The writing, called *hieroglyphics*, was done by priests (*glyph* means write or carve and *hiero* means sacred). With hieroglyphics it was possible to write about anything—no matter how abstract—and to refer clearly and unmistakably to a particular person.

Great as this advance was, hieroglyphics was nevertheless clumsy. In order to write, one had to learn to make three or four thousand different pictures. Don't forget, there were separate pictures for each syllable in a word. Writing—just the sheer physical act of writing—was a profession. To become a scribe required years of intense study.

The Third Stage—The Alphabet

It was not until the third stage, our present alphabetic stage, that real writing became possible. All we know about the unknown genius (or group of geniuses) who invented the alphabet is that he or she spoke a Hebrew language. The creator of the alphabet discovered that despite the hundreds and thousands of different words that people used when they spoke, they employed only a limited number of actual sounds—some twenty-two, in fact. All words were simply combinations of this limited number of sounds.

Although the discovery of the twenty-two sounds may seem childishly simple, it was indeed a remarkable feat of analysis, and, furthermore, it gave birth to a brilliant idea: If there were only twenty-two sounds, why not make a picture to represent each sound? Learning to write would then become the comparatively simple task of learning to make twenty-two pictures.

In choosing the pictures, our unknown inventor displayed true genius. He chose pictures that would immediately suggest the individual sounds they were to represent. For example, the Hebrew word for camel is *gimel*; to indicate the sound *g* our scribe drew a picture of the hump of a camel ⌒. To signify the sound *b* he made an outline of a house, because house in Hebrew is *bet*. Similarly, a wavy line〰 to indicate water (*mayim*, in Hebrew) stood for the sound *m*. The symbols that stood for the twenty-two sounds could be grouped in different ways to make words, which, after all, are merely specific combinations of sounds. These symbols, of course, are what we now call the letters of the alphabet.

Although the inventor of the alphabet spoke Hebrew, we credit the Phoenicians with perfecting the alphabet and spreading it throughout the world. The Phoenicians lived just north of the Hebrews, on a narrow strip of land hugging the coast. The two peoples were cousins; their languages were practically identical. The Phoenicians were the great traders of the ancient world, carrying their wares to all known parts. They keenly felt the need of a simple way of keeping records of their many transactions, and so they used and perfected and then exported the alphabet in their dealings with the rest of the world.

The invention of the alphabet—that marvelous instrument by which the sounds that come from a person's mouth are written down for others to read—was unquestionably one of the greatest inventions in the history of mankind, and one of the greatest triumphs of human intellect.

The Greeks Learn to Use the Alphabet

The first great nation the Phoenicians came upon as they traveled westward were the Greeks. Impressed by the power and beauty of the Greek language, the Phoenicians were utterly amazed to discover that this intelligent and gifted race could not read or write.

Once the Phoenicians explained the idea of writing, the Greeks were eager to learn, so the Phoenicians taught them the twenty-two letters of their alphabet. The Greeks began to write their language with the strange-looking letters, but they soon ran into a problem—there were no symbols for vowel sounds. Since the Phoenicians did not use vowels in writing, their alphabet did not account for the sounds of *a, e, i, o, u*.

The Greeks Need Pictures for the Vowels

In Greek, as in other European languages (including, of course, English), the meaning of a word depends upon vowels as well as consonants. Different vowels used with the same consonants can create words with altogether different meanings. Since you are probably not familiar with Greek, we will illustrate this in English. Let us take the two consonants *r* and *d*. See what can happen:

R ai D

R ea D y

R ee D

R   e   D

R   i   D

R   i   D e

R oa D

R   o   D

R   u   D e

By changing the vowels used with these two consonants, we get many, and mostly unrelated, words. There is a world of difference between *reed*, *red*, and *ride*, and it would be extremely difficult—if not impossible—to read a sentence made up only of consonants. The Greeks simply had to have vowel letters.

Now let's look at Hebrew. Take the word *kadosh*, which means holy. We can change the vowels of these consonants in many different ways, just as we changed the vowels of "r . . . . d," and we will also get many words. However, all the words coming from *kadosh*, essentially convey the same idea, namely "holiness."

kadosh	A holy person
kodesh, kidusha	holiness
kadish	The mourner's prayer

kiddush   Prayer declaring the
                         Sabbath night to be holy

Thus, people writing the Hebrew language could get along without any vowel signs for many centuries. It was quite impossible to do the same with Greek or English.

The Hebrew vowel signs used today were invented quite late, in the seventh century.

The Greeks Add Vowel Letters

The Greeks cleverly solved the problem of the missing vowel sounds. Since the Hebrew alphabet included several sounds that did not exist in Greek, the Greeks used the superfluous letters to indicate vowels. For example, the Hebrew letter *ayin* represents a deep gutteral sound that does not exist in the Greek language. So the Greeks took the *ayin*, which in old Hebrew was written like an *o*, and used it— you can easily guess—for the vowel sound *o*, which value it still has in English today. In this fashion, the Hebrew *alef* became *a*, the *hay* became *e* and so on.

This adaptation by the Greeks of otherwise useless letters for necessary vowel sounds was a great step forward in the evolution of written language. It enabled the alphabet to pass from the exclusive possession of the Semitic people and to become a useful instrument in writing Indo-European languages. Thus, in a certain sense, the Greeks can be regarded as co-creators of our present alphabet.

Greek used to be written as Hebrew is, from right to left. When the Greeks began to write from left to right, they turned many letters around. If you turn around some of the old Hebrew letters, you will see that they are almost identical with modern English letters:

 is old Hebrew *alef*.	Set it up straight; it is an *a*.
 is old Hebrew *daled*.	Turn it sideways and curve it slightly; it is a *d*.
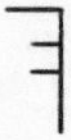 is old Hebrew *hay*.	Turn it around; it is an *e*.
 is old Hebrew *zayin*.	Turn it around; it is an *z*.
 is old Hebrew *mem*.	It resembles the English *m*.
 is old Hebrew *ayin*.	It is the same as the English *o*.
 is old Hebrew *quf*.	It resembles the English *q*.
 is old Hebrew *tav*.	It is practically identical to the English *t*.
 is old Hebrew *shin*.	Turn it sideways and curve; it will become an *s*.

Once the alphabet was invented, the astonishing ease of this new way of writing became apparent to all. Other systems—like the cuneiform writing of the Assyrians and the men of Elba, and the hieroglyphic writing of the Egyptians —simply died out. In fact, it was not until the late eighteenth and nineteenth centuries that these early forms of writing were deciphered.

In 1797, Jean François Champollion discovered the Rosetta Stone, which contained writing in Greek and hieroglyphics. Within a few years, Champollion worked out the key for reading ancient Egyptian, and thus founded the science of Egyptology. Understanding the writing of the ancient Egyptians provided the first clue to understanding their civilization.

In 1840, Henry Rawlinson, an Englishman, examined the Behistun Rock, on which were inscriptions in ancient Assyrian and in Persian. By working from the Persian, a known language, Rawlinson sought to decipher the unknown cuneiform. After intensive study, he emerged with the key to practically the entire cuneiform alphabet. With this new information, the science of Assyriology was born.

When people first began to speak, they could communicate with their contemporaries; when they learned how to write, they could then communicate with their descendants.

The Anglo-Saxon Language Evolves from the Indo-European Language

Long before the birth of Christ, there was a group of tribes that spoke a common language. Although we do not know exactly where these tribes lived, they were probably located somewhere in southeastern Europe. From this parent group, various tribes broke off and wandered away at different times: the Greeks migrated to Greece; the Romans settled around Rome; the Germans in Germany; the Persians in Persia (now Iran); and the ancestors of the Hindus in present-day India. All these different peoples spoke widely variant forms of the single, very ancient Indo-European language. This Indo-European language was the mother of large numbers of language families.

The ancestors of the present-day English were the Anglo-Saxons, Germanic tribes that had lived in northern Germany near the North Sea. Around the year 450, the Anglo-Saxons migrated from Germany and settled a new country, which they named "Anglo-land," or England.

These Germanic peoples, of course, also brought with them their language—again, a variation of the parent Indo-European language. Around the first century, a highly regular shift in the pronunciation of a number of sounds had taken place among the German-speaking tribes.

What were these sounds and how did they change?

Grimm's Law

The nineteenth-century German, Jacob Grimm, is best known for the vast collection of fairy tales that he, along with his brother, gathered and wrote down. But Jacob Grimm was also, oddly enough, one of the world's great linguistic scholars. He formulated what the world has since known as *Grimm's Law*, which describes a curious characteristic of Germanic languages, and thus, of our own English. Here, we will be describing only one section of Grimm's Law.

Plosives

There are a number of sounds in our alphabet that we call *plosives*. When we make these sounds, there is an extremely tiny, but quite definite, explosion of the breath. There are six of these plosives, divided into two groups: *k, p, t* are voiceless plosives; that is, when you make these sounds, you hardly hear any voice. The voiced plosives are *b, d, g*; when you say them, you hear a certain rumbling sound.

If you put your finger on your throat while making the sounds of the first group (*k, p, t*), you will not feel any vibrations. When, however, you make the sounds of the second group (*b, d, g*), you will feel at once the rumbling in your throat, the vibration of your vocal cords.

Incidentally, these six sounds are also called *stops*. Unlike the sounds *s, r,* or *l,* for example, which you can continue saying on and on as long as you have breath, once you make the plosive or stop sounds, you simply have to stop. You can, of course, repeat the sound over again, but you can't continue it in one breath. Just say out loud any word which ends with a plosive sound—the word *kit*, for example. Now do the same with a word which doesn't end in a stop—for example, *kiss*—and continue to make the final sound until you run of breath.

Around the first century, the voiceless plosives *k*, *p*, *t* in the Germanic language group shifted, and the

> **k** sound became **h**
> **p** sound became **f**
> **t** sound became **th**

Bearing in mind that English is a Germanic language (the Anglo-Saxons were, remember, a Germanic tribe) and also that English borrowed an enormous number of words from Latin, it will follow that our language contains many doublets—two words having the same ancestry or origin. However, the words coming from Anglo-Saxon, a Germanic language, reflect the shift indicated by Grimm's Law, while the later words, of Latin origin, do not.

Let's look at some examples of Grimm's Law in action.

Latin K—Often Written C—Became English H

The Latin word *centum* (pronounced "kentum") became the English HUNDRED. In English, we pronounce *centum* with a soft *c* (like *s*), and we also have many words coming from it, such as CENT (one hundredth of a dollar), CENTURY (one hundred years), CENTENNIAL, etc.

The Latin *cornu* (a musical instrument) has become the English HORN. The English word CORONET, however, has come directly from the Latin.

Canem in Latin is dog. With the shift of the hard *c* (the *k* sound) to *h*, we have the English word HOUND. But we also have, directly from the Latin *canem*, CANINE (doglike) and KENNEL (a place where dogs are kept).

The Latin root *cord* has as its English cognate the word HEART. CARDIAC, which comes directly from the Latin, means "relating to the heart."

The Latin *cremate* corresponds to the English cognate HEARTH, part of the floor on which a fire is made. CREMATE is also an English word meaning to burn a dead body.

Latin P Became English F

Ped is Latin for "foot." With the Germanic shift from *p* to *f*, we have our English word FOOT. But we also have a whole group of words—all having to do with "foot"—which came directly from the Latin *ped*: PEDAL (a lever activated by the foot), PEDESTAL (the foot of a column), PEDESTRIAN (a person who travels on foot), TRIPOD (three feet), OCTOPUS (eight feet).

The Latin *plenus* became the English FULL. Coming directly from the Latin *plenum*, we have the word PLENTY.

The Latin *pater* became the English FATHER. PATERNAL (fatherly) comes directly from the Latin.

The Latin *pro* became the English FOR (with the last two letters changing place).

The Latin *nepos* became the English NEPHEW. Showing favoritism to your relatives is called NEPOTISM.

The Latin word *pecus* (capital or property) corresponds to the English word FEE (money paid for services rendered). PECUNIARY, the English word of Latin origin, means "relating to money."

The Greek *pyro* has as its English cognate the word FIRE. A PYROMANIAC is a person with a mad passion for setting fires.

The Latin *pisc* is the English FISH. Coming directly from the Latin is PISCATORIAL (having to do with fish).

Latin T Became English TH

The Latin root *dent* became the English TOOTH. Directly from the Latin, we have DENTIST, DENTAL, ORTHODONTIST, DENTIFRICE.

The Greek *tri* became the English THREE. We also have TRIPOD (three feet), TRIENNIAL (every three years), TRICYCLE (THREE WHEELS), etc.

The Latin *tumor* (a swelling) corresponds to the English cognate THUMB, which of course looks like a swollen finger. Our English words TUMOR and TUMESCENCE (swelling) have entered the language directly from the Latin.

The Latin *tenus* (stretched out) has as its English cognate the word THIN, but it is also the direct ancestor of the word TENUOUS meaning slight.

The Shift of the Voiced Plosives

The second group of plosives—*b*, *d*, *g*—are the voiced or loud-sounded plosives. In the Germanic languages, the voiced plosives underwent a shift to their unvoiced counterparts, namely:

b became **p**
d became **t**
g became **k**

Latin B Became English P

The Latin *labium* became the English LIP. LABIAL in English means having to do with the lips.

The Latin *lubricum* became—with an *s* added to the beginning—the English word SLIPPING. From *lubricum* we also got LUBRICATE.

Latin D Became English T

As discussed earlier, the Latin root *dent* became the English TOOTH; *ped* became FOOT; *cord* became HEART.

The Latin *edere* has become the English word EAT. EDIBLE comes directly from the Latin.

The Latin *duo* corresponds to the English TWO.

THE LATIN *dicere* (to plan, to say) has as its English cognate TEACH. The word DICTATE comes from the Latin.

Latin G Became English K (often written as C)

The Latin *granum* became the English CORN. We also have the words GRANARY and, of course, GRAIN.

The Latin *genu* has as its English cognate the word KNEE. GENUFLECT (to bend the knee) comes directly from the Latin (we don't sound the *k* now, but at one time it was heard clearly).

The Latin *genus* corresponds to the English KIN or KIND, and it has also come directly into our language as GENUS.

The Latin *agelr* (a field for farming) has as its doublet the English ACRE (a measure of farming land).

To Summarize Grimm's Law:

LATIN		ENGLISH
P	became	F
T	became	TH
K	became	H
B	became	D
D	became	T
G	became	R

New Words Come From Old Words

The language spoken by the Anglo-Saxons—called either Anglo-Saxon or Old English—looks like a foreign language to us. Indeed, it is studied in colleges as a foreign language, just like Greek or Latin. Below is a Biblical passage written in Old English, with a modern English translation above it. This will give you an idea how much English has changed since its inception.

> *And   going   into   the   house they   found*
> And gangende intō *þam hūse   hī gemētton
>
> *the   child with   Mary   its   mother*
> *þaett cild   mid Marian hys mēder
>
> (MATTHEW 2:11)

* þ or *thorn* was the Anglo-Saxon letter for *th*.

Although we will never know exactly how many words were used in this ancient Anglo-Saxon language, linguistic scholars believe the number to be about a hundred thousand.

In the written literature that has come down to us, there are no more than fifty thousand words. We can easily assume that at least another fifty thousand were in oral use, but did not survive in written form.

The English we use today includes about a million words. How did our language grow in the past fifteen thousand years?

Throughout the world, languages have increased in size and usefulness by following certain standard patterns. We will trace many of the ways languages grow in this and the following chapters.

Simple Combinations

A rather simple, but fruitful, way of word-building is by combination, that is, by putting together two words—sometimes even three—to make a new word.

It is a simple trick but highly effective. Take, for example, a HUNTSMAN: he is a *man* who *hunts*. A BOOKMARK is something that *marks* your place in a *book*. A BEDROOM is a *room* in which you will usually find a *bed*. A FORTNIGHT is a period of two weeks, or *fourteen nights*.

A pot is a *pot* and luck is *luck*; but if you come unexpectedly to a friend's house near mealtime, he may invite you to take POTLUCK, that is, to share whatever by chance or good *luck* may be in the *pot* on the stove.

When the fortunes of war went against his master, a TURNCOAT would *turn* his *coat* inside out so that he would not be recognized as belonging to his master's following or army.

The TELLTALE lipstick marks on a young man's cheek, as he emerges from a dark room, *tell tales* of what went on behind the closed door.

All these combinations are rather simple. With a moment or two of thought, their origins are all obvious. But sometimes the combinations are ancient—formed many centuries ago in different lands. To work them out requires a keen eye and an inquiring mind. For example:

ALARM   *All arme* are two Italian words which mean "To arms! Get your weapons!" In other words, it is a phrase which ALARMS others to danger. (Of course, it is a far cry from this desperate, urgent call to the ring of the alarm clock in the morning.)

ALPHABET   *Aleph* and *bet* were the first two letters of the old Hebrew/Phoenician ALPHABET.

BONFIRE   In the Middle Ages, the victims of war or plague were often too numerous to be buried individually. Instead, their *bones* were burned in a huge *fire*. Today, happily, BONFIRES serve less grisly purposes.

CURFEW   In French, *couvre feu* means "cover the fire." At a certain hour in the evening a bell rang, signaling that it was time to cover (put out) the fire and go to sleep.

DAISY   The yellow center of this flower reminded the Anglo-Saxons of an extremely tiny sun; in other words, it resembled the *day's eye*, or DAISY.

DANDELION   The sharply jagged leaves of this flower caused the French to call it *dent de lion*, meaning "teeth of the lion."

GOSPEL   *Good spel* meant the "good message of the coming of Christ." The original *od* fell out to yield the present word GOSPEL.

HIPPOPOTAMUS   When the Greeks first saw this strange beast lolling in the waters of the Nile, they were bewildered. But they quickly rallied and called the enormous creature the horse (*hippo*) of the river (*potamus*).

LADY/LORD   *Loaf*, (bread) plus *dige*, (kneader) have combined to form LADY, or one who kneads bread. The Anglo-Saxon women were the "loaf kneaders" of the household. The same *loaf* combined with *ward* (guardian) to form LORD, the guardian of the food supply.

LONGSHOREMEN   An example of more than two words combining to form a third is LONGSHOREMEN, which originates from the *men* who worked *along the shore*, loading and unloading ships.

NEIGHBORS   The first part of this word comes from an old Anglo-Saxon word for NIGH, or NEAR, while the second part is from the Anglo-Saxon word for "farmer," *bor*. (Sad to relate, but *bor* is also the root of the word BOOR, a rude, uncultured person.) Although today, we think of a NEIGHBOR as someone in the next apartment or the next building, a long time ago, your NEIGHBOR was simply "the farmer who was nigh." (Incidentally, the BOERS of South Africa were so named because they were farmers.)

Blending

A somewhat different combination of words is called blending. In ordinary combinations, we usually see two or three whole words put together. (A KEYHOLE is a *hole* for the *key*. A BOOKSELLER is one who *sells books*.) Blending is a more intimate fusion, in which we combine the first part of one word and the second part of another word.

For example: BRUNCH is a blend of *br*eakfast and *l*u*nch*.

America is a nation on wheels, but after a number of hours of driving, even the most determined motorist must stop for food and rest. To accommodate this need, hotels that cater especially to people traveling by car were built across the country. A happy blend was created: MOTEL, coming from *mo*tor *h*o*tel*.

The air in Los Angeles is often filled with a combination of *sm*oke and f*og*, or SMOG.

When a person is DUMBFOUNDED, he is actually struck *dumb* and con*founded*.

FLAUNT is a blend of *fl*out and *v*a*unt*.

When you GRUMBLE, you are both *gr*owling and *r*u*mbling*.

BLURT is a blend of *bl*ow and sp*urt*.

Quiz 1

ARE YOU A GOOD
WORD DETECTIVE?

*Fill in the blanks with the proper
combination word or combination-word element.*

1. The first meal of the day is called *breakfast* because
   with it we _____ our _____ .

2. Something which is quite silly, which makes *no sense*, is
   called _____ .

3. A *kidnapper* was one who seized children, who
   _____ them.

4. One who takes care of *sheep* is called a _____ .

5. Shipshape means "neat, orderly, trim," the way things
   are arranged on a _____ .

6. To *waylay* a person is to *lie* in *wait* for him, actually to
   lie in his _____ .

7. We say *welcome* to express our pleasure at a person's
   arrival; we are telling him, it is _____ that he has
   come.

Answers on page 180

Words Are Clipped and Shortened

Many words in English have shortened or clipped forms. People are often too lazy to say a long word, particularly if they think they'll be understood if they use a shorter version of the word.

We hardly ever refer to the room in which science experiments are conducted as the *laboratory*; we almost always say LAB. Similarly, we play basketball in a GYM instead of *gymnasium*; we use the PHONE, not *telephone*; we get the FLU, not *influenza*. People visit the ZOO, not the *zoological gardens*, and women wear BRAS, not *brassieres*. We take a PHOTO (*photograph*) and write a MEMO (*memorandum*). We buy GAS (*gasoline*) for our AUTO (*automobile*).

All these abbreviated words are clear and simple, and usually both the long and short forms of the word are well known. But sometimes the short form is used so completely to the exclusion of the longer form that the original form becomes unknown. For example:

BUS   Very few people remember that the word BUS was originally *omnibus*.

CANTER   The unhurried pace of the pilgrims winding their way to the religious shrine at *Canterbury* has come to be called a CANTER.

30

DRAWING ROOM   After formal dinners, the ladies would go to what is called a DRAWING ROOM, although no drawing was done there. The linguistic puzzle is solved when we understand that the name is a shortened form of *withdrawing room*. The women would with*draw* to another *room*, leaving the men to smoke their cigars.

FAN   Few people who have witnessed the frenzied enthusiasm of a sports crowd will doubt that the word FAN is short for *fanatic*, or zealot.

FENCE/FENCER/FENDER   These are all shortened forms of *defense*. The FENCE around a house is a sort of *defense*. The FENCE who receives stolen goods acts in *defense* of the criminal. A FENCER *defends* himself against attack, just as a FENDER *defends* a car in case of collision.

GIN   Eli Whitney's cotton GIN is just a shortened form of *engine*. The alcoholic drink has an entirely different origin: GIN is short for *Geneva*, the city where it was made.

GOODBYE   This word (which is often shortened to just plain BYE) is itself an abbreviated way of saying *God be with you*.

LUSCIOUS   A short form of *delicious*.

MEND   A short form of *amend*.

MOB   This succinct word comes from *mobile vulgar*, the excitable, fickle people.

PANTS   Now used exclusively instead of the longer original, *pantaloons*.

PEP   When you think of "zest" as the meaning of the word PEP, it makes sense that it should come from the sharp spice, *pepper*.

PEST   Now simply an annoying person, PEST originally came from the dreaded *pestilence*, a fatal epidemic.

SPEND   An abbreviated form of *dispense*.

STILL   As an apparatus used to produce alcohol, STILL is short for *distillation*, the process of evaporation and condensation by which the alcohol is purified.

STRESS   A short form of the word *distress*.

TAXICAB   What person calling for a TAXI or CAB (themselves shortened versions of TAXICAB) knows that its full name is *taximeter cabriolet*? There is a clear connection between taxes and a taxi: each taxi has a meter that measures off the tax you must pay for enjoying the use of the vehicle.

TEND   The longer, original version is *attend*.

VAN   The short form of two entirely different words: from *caravan* we have the VAN that is a truck; from *vanguard* we have the VAN that means the group in the front or lead position.

WIG   Long ago, people wore *periwigs* (from the French *perruque*); today we simply wear WIGS.

Quiz 2

ARE YOU A GOOD WORD DETECTIVE?

Fill in the blanks with the proper short or long form of the word in italics.

1. A short form of the word *fable*—a story that is not literally true—is a _____.

2. We say *fortnight* and we mean a period of two weeks. It is actually a short way of saying _____ nights.

3. *Never* is simply a short way of saying the two words

   _____ _____ .

4. The word *pest* in a sentence, for example, "Don't make a pest of yourself," is a very weak, short form of the word that means a fatal epidemic, a contagious disease. The word is _____ .

5. *Electrocution* is short for execution by _____ .

6. *Flu* is short for _____ .

7. It used to be called *revolving* pistol because the loaded barrel, the little chambers containing the cartridge, would turn about. We have dropped one word and now it is called _____ .

Answers on page 180

Why Lions Roar, Bees Buzz, and Brooks Babble

Imagine a time many thousands of years ago. A man comes running out of the forest, breathless, wild-eyed, white with fear. He has just seen a lion in the woods and heard its deep-throated roar; he has barely escaped its ferocious claws. Now in the village, the man wants to warn his friends of the danger that lurks in the forest. So he screams out to them, imitating the lion's roar: "*ri—ri—ri!*" They hear and they understand.

The man has invented the word ROAR.

Picture little children playing at the edge of a clearing in front of their home. Suddenly, their mother spots a snake approaching them, poised to strike. Horror-stricken, she HISSES out to them a sharp warning sound: "*Sssss!*" The children understand, and run to safety.

ROAR and HISS are two examples of onomatopoeic words; that is, words formed by imitating natural sounds. *Onomatopoeia* is a clumsy word for a neat concept: man's attempt to imitate the sounds of nature. Some of our most beautiful and poetic words arose out of these fumbling efforts to reproduce what was heard in the jungle, forest, and field. Man heard bees BUZZ and brooks BABBLING. He heard CLANGING, HOWLING, YELLING, WAILING, etc.

Describing the phenomena of life by imitating the

sounds they produce is only natural. Thus, the onomato-poeic words are among the most ancient in any language; English has an unusually large number of them. Onomato-poeic words are the only words in each language whose origin is not the least puzzling.

Man himself is responsible for a variety of fairly strange noises, which language reproduces more or less exactly. When a man has a cold, he will SNEEZE, and might GARGLE his throat. You can hear the sound of BUBBLING liquid in both the words GARGLE and GURGLE. If he is in real pain, a man may GROAN or MOAN.

A cheerful person may WHISTLE or HUM or GIGGLE or TIT-TER. The aroma of frying eggs and bacon SIZZLING on the griddle may cause him to SMACK his lips. If he eats too fast, he may get the HICCUPS or he may BURP. When asleep, he may SNORE, to the gentle TICKING of his bedside clock.

Words for sounds made in the animal world are frequently onomatopoeic. Wild animals can GROWL or SNARL. Cows MOO, donkeys BRAY, and horses NEIGH. Dogs BARK and cats MEOW. Birds CHIRP, owls HOOT, hens CACKLE or CLUCK, and geese HONK. Frogs CROAK. Both the CROW and the CUCKOO are so named because of the sounds they make.

Mechanical objects have also produced onomatopoeic words. We speak of the HUM, the CLATTER, the WHIR of machinery; the CLICKING of typewriter keys; the WHIZZING of a car going by.

There is also a group of onomatopoeic words denoting soft sounds or silence: HUSH, WHISPER, RUSTLE. And how many times has someone told you to keep quiet by saying, "Not another PEEP out of you."

Even the word QUACK, used to denote a medical charlatan, is onomatopoeic: long ago, self-styled doctors hawking their miraculous healing potions at county fairs sounded just like ducks QUACKING.

Prattle Words

Related to the onomatopoeic words are prattle words— which derive from the first and easiest sounds for a baby to make. Prattle words are interesting because they are pretty much the same all over the world.

The simplest sound for a baby to make is to send breath through its lips and utter "*ma-ma-ma*." All over the world, mothers eagerly listening to their infants say "*ma-ma-ma*" show their pleasure at hearing these first sounds. The child enjoys the mother's reaction and repeats the same sounds with the mother responding each time. The "*ma-ma*" sounds became a worldwide signal for MOTHER: in German—*mutter*; in Latin—*mater*; in French—*mère*; in Hebrew—*imma*, and so on.

The next sound a baby makes is usually something like "*ba-ba*." This became PAPA, in English; *pater*, in Latin; *vater*, in German; *père, in French; abba*, in Hebrew. The prattle sound "*ba-ba*" is also the origin of the word BABY.

The third sound is "*da-da-da*." The proud father would say, "The baby is calling me," and so the prattle sound "*da-da*" became the pet name for father—that is, DADDY.

Quiz 3

ARE YOU A GOOD
WORD DETECTIVE?

Fill in the blanks with the proper onomatopoeic word.

1. The _____ of the wagon across the old wooden bridge could be heard far upstream.

2. The valiant little engine _____ up the steep hill.

3. The _____ of the crows in the early morning startled the visiting city boy into wakefulness.

4. The children _____ with delight when the _____ pigs were herded into the pen.

5. A _____ of fear pierced the night silence.

6. Rice crispies go _____, _____, and _____.

7. The hot-rodder revved up the engine, and _____ down the highway at top speed.

Answers on page 180

Words Come from Names

Words come from the names of places and people. Often, products bear the names of the places where they are grown or manufactured, or were invented: The BAYONET was invented in the French city *Bayonne*; SCALLIONS grow wildly in *Ashkelon*, Israel; the bright blue dye INDIGO comes from *India*; the fabric DAMASK from *Damascus*, Syria; and MUSLIN from *Mosul*, Iraq.

Likewise, people who invent new objects or processes may lend their own names to their discoveries: PASTEURIZATION comes from the name of the chemist who devised the process, Louis *Pasteur*. Words also derive from the names of people who were famous for a particular reason: The German KAISER and the Russian CZAR come from the name of an earlier leader, the celebrated Julius *Caesar*.

There is often a simple, direct translation from the original name to the word it spawns: CHAMPAGNE comes from the French province *Champagne*; SARDINES come from *Sardinia*, an island off Italy; SUEDE comes from *Sweden*; GAUZE from *Gaza*, Israel; TANGERINES from the North African city of *Tangiers*. Sometimes, however, the process is a bit more complicated, and yields an interesting story.

Below are some examples of words that derive from the names of places:

BIBLE This word comes from the Phoenician city of

Byblos, in a somewhat roundabout fashion. The Phoenicians were the great merchant princes of the ancient Middle East, trading with many parts of the known world. Around 3000 B.C., they enjoyed a brisk trade relationship with Egypt, from which they imported papyrus plants, among other things. After processing the plant, the Phoenicians sold it as writing material. (*Papyrus* is the origin of the word PAPER.)

The Greeks imported papyrus from Byblos, and they wrote all their books on it. They called the material "byblos" after the Phoenician city. *Byblos* became the Greek word for BOOK and, of course, for the book par excellence—the BIBLE.

BEDLAM   The Hospital of St. Mary of *Bethlehem* was an insane asylum in London. Wild cries made by its unfortunate inmates echoed in the street. From this constant noise arose the word BEDLAM (the *th* sound in *Bethlehem* was slurred into a *d*).

CANARY   When the Romans first came upon the islands now called the Canary Islands, they found a large number of wild dogs. The called the islands *Insulae Canariae*, or "islands of the dogs." (From the Latin *canis*, meaning "dog," also come the words CANINE and KENNEL.) Not until much later were the beautiful yellow finches of the islands discovered and named CANARIES.

COLOGNE   *Cologne*, Germany was established by the Romans, who gave the city its name, which means the *colony*. Much later, prefumed toilet water was manufactured there, and the word COLOGNE came to be used for all such fragrances.

COPPER   This story actually begins with the name of the island of *Cyprus*, which was so named in ancient times because of the *cypress* trees that grew there in great abundance. Actually, the ancients pronounced Cyprus with a hard *c*, that is, *Kyprus*. Much later, a reddish-brown metal was discovered on this island, and as it was very useful, the metal was sent from Cyprus to all the lands of the Mediterranean. The Romans called it *aes cuprium*, which simply meant "the metal from Cyprus." This was then shortened to the familiar word *copper.* (By the way, KIPPERED herring gets its name from its copper color.)

CORDOVAN   People in the city of *Córdoba*, Spain tanned a leather that was excellent and durable. Thus, this leather was called CORDOVAN, and to this day, it is a highly prized leather used for shoes and bookbinding.

MARATHON   In 490 B.C., the Greeks won a decisive victory against the Persians in the city of *Marathon*. A runner ran from the battle scene twenty-six miles to Athens, where he cried out, "We have won! The Persians are defeated." Deriving its name from the battle-site and its meaning from the runner's feat, the word MARATHON has come to mean any feat of great endurance.

MEANDER   In ancient Greece, there was a winding, wandering river, which continually curved from side to side. From its name, *Menderes*, we get the word MEANDER, which means to wander about without a fixed purpose.

MILLINERY   Women's hats of striking beauty were made in the city of *Milan*, Italy. MILLINERY became the word for women's hats.

PALACE   On the *Palatine* Hill in Rome, wealthy Romans built large, beautiful homes, which today are known as PALACES.

TURKEY   This big, luscious fowl was originally believed to come from the land of *Turkey*. Interestingly, the Turks returned the compliment by calling it the American bird!

TURQUOISE   This semiprecious stone also gets its name from *Turkey*, where it can be found in great supply.

Names from People

Popular first names are often used to indicate sex. From the name *Thomas* come the expressions TOM TURKEY (a male turkey), and TOMBOY (a girl who acts like a boy). From the name *Anne* comes the expression for a female goat, "an Anne goat," or NANNY GOAT, while the male of the species, the BILLY GOAT, derives from *Billy*, the nickname for William.

Classical mythology has proven a rich source for words deriving from names: HERCULEAN means having the strength of the hero *Hercules*; MARTIAL, meaning warlike, comes from *Mars*, the god of war; MUSIC and MUSEUM derive from the *Muses*, the nine daughters of Jupiter who presided over the arts; and VOLCANOES were believed to be the gigantic workshops of the Roman god of fire and metalworking, *Vulcanus*.

Below are several of the derivative words that have immortalized other people:

BOYCOTT   In 1879, there was a terrible famine in Ireland. Despite this hardship, a landlord's agent named Charles *Boycott* cruelly refused to reduce rents. The agent was therefore ostracized by the community; people turned their backs on him, refusing to speak to him. Thus arose the verb BOYCOTT, which means to refuse to buy, sell, or use.

CHAUVINISM   A French soldier named Nicholas *Chauvin* persisted in praising Napoleon even after the senseless killing of French youths in the Napoleonic Wars. Chauvin's friends ridiculed his stubborn, blind patriotism, which came to be known as CHAUVINISM.

COLOSSAL   The inhabitants of Rhodes, an island in the Mediterranean, won a great victory over the invading Macedonians. In gratitude, the Rhodians erected an enormous statue to the sun god around 285 B.C. Named the *Colossus of Rhodes*, the bronze statue was 105 feet high, and became one of the seven wonders of the ancient world. Hence, anything characterized by extreme bulk, strength, or effect is said to be COLOSSAL.

EPICURE   The Greek philosopher *Epicuros* believed that happiness and pleasure were the only goals of life. Today an EPICURE is one who pursues only pleasure.

GUILLOTINE   During the reign of terror following the French Revolution, a physician named Joseph *Guillotin* recommended that a gigantic knife be dropped on the necks of the people to be executed. This speedy, efficient, and fairly painless method of execution is still used in France today. In honor of the French doctor, the device was called the GUILLOTINE.

LYNCH   Another form of execution—*not* sanctioned by the government—is LYNCHING, which derives from the name of a Virginian, Charles *Lynch*. This man organized his neighbors into an informal police group to punish those who he believed were guilty. Today, anyone put to death without a formal, fair trial is said to have been LYNCHED.

MAUSOLEUM   When the powerful king *Mausolus* died, his

disconsolate queen commanded that a large, beautiful building be constructed over his grave. This MAUSOLEUM was one of the seven wonders of the ancient world.

PLATONIC The Greek philosopher *Plato* believed love should be spiritual and not physical. This type of love has come to be called PLATONIC.

SANDWICH Lord *Sandwich* was a passionate card player, sometimes playing all night long. As he had no time to sit down to a meal, he would order food brought to him. He would ask for two slices of bread with a slab of meat in between—in other words, a SANDWICH.

SLAVE The *Slavs* are a group of people who have dwelled for thousands of years in the lands that are now Poland and White Russia or Belorussia. Their land was constantly conquered by invaders; the people were subjugated and compelled to work for masters. From the name *Slav* comes our word SLAVE.

TAWDRY *St. Audrey's* fair became famous for the cheap, low-quality jewelry that was sold there. TAWDRY now describes any cheap, shoddy goods.

VANDAL The *Vandals*, a German tribe, helped bring the Roman Empire to a close. They sacked the city of Rome, stripping it of everything valuable. To this day, people who senselessly destroy valuable property are called VANDALS.

Quiz 4

ARE YOU A GOOD
WORD DETECTIVE?

Fill in the blanks with the proper name or name-word.

1. *Gypsies* actually came from India, but because they sojourned so long in _____, they were called *gypsies.*

2. *Ceres* was the ancient Roman goddess of the grain crop. From her we get our familiar word _____.

3. The Greek god Jupiter had nine daughters called *Muses*, who presided over the various arts. One major art named after the *Muses* is _____.

4. The building that houses various kinds of art is called a

   _____ .

5. *Indian* in English means both "native American" and "inhabitant of India," all because Christopher Columbus blundered and believed he had arrived in _____.

6. *Indigo*, a blue powder obtained from plants, has been used for thousands of years as a dye. It comes from

   _____ .

7. *Suede* leather comes from _____.

8. *Cinder* means "ash." To incinerate means "to turn into ashes." In the fairy tale, the young and beautiful maiden who served as a household drudge, cleaning ashes from the hearth, was called _____.

9. The Roman fire god was called *Vulcanus*. Certain mountains made weird noises, and belched smoke and fire. The ancients thought these mountains most certainly contained the gigantic forge of the god *Vulcanus*, so they called these mountains by the name _____.

Answers on page 180

Why Tables Have "Legs" and People Feel "Blue"

How odd it is, when you come to think of it, that tables should have *legs* and people feel *blue*. How is it possible for a color to be *loud* or a question *hard?* Can colors be *noisy?*

All this brings us to one of the most pervasive, fruitful, and subtle ways of word building. It is generally called the figurative use of words, and simply means that the original meaning is shifted or extended to mean something else vaguely related to the original. We are so accustomed to this process of word building, that we hardly ever stop to analyze what we are saying. Yet by this simple trick, we have actually doubled and sometimes tripled our vocabulary.

There is little doubt that in very ancient days every word was physical: that is, every word described a concrete object that could be felt, seen, heard, tasted, or smelled. Every root word expressed a physical act of primitive people. This was only natural. Words for physical actions were the ones most desperately needed for the survival of primitive humans.

But as the years went by, life became more complex, and ancient man felt the need for additional words. He wanted words to express ideas that were not physical at all. He wanted to talk about things that could not be compre-

hended by the five senses. He wanted to pass moral judgments, to speak of religious ideals, to make intellectual dis-
tinctions. He wanted to describe emotional states. He needed
more words.

The human mind, then as now, was fairly lazy. Instead
of creating new words for these non-physical concepts, ancient humans simply used the old stock of physical words.
This linguistic laziness was somewhat justified by the fact
that within the limited stock of physical words, primitive
humans could always find one word that suggested exactly
what it was they wanted to express.

Did someone want to say that one member of the tribe
was outstanding or important, that he had made significant
contributions to the welfare of all? The adjectives BIG and
GREAT immediately came to mind. And so today, when we
say, "He is a big man," or "She is a great woman," we are
hardly ever referring to physical size.

Early woman wanted to indicate a person who dealt
fairly with her fellows; she needed a word for honesty.
There was something about a straight line that suggested
honesty and trustworthiness. And so, STRAIGHT came to
mean, in addition to its physical sense, "honest" or "upright."

Early man also needed a word to express what he felt
when something unpleasant happened to him—when he
was humiliated, defeated, insulted. There came to his mind
the taste of a bitter fruit, and so BITTER came to describe the
feeling produced by frustration or defeat.

Thus were old words used in new ways.

When a woman received a friendly welcome from one of
her friends, there was something about the gesture that reminded her of the friendly warmth of a comfortable fire.
And so today, we speak of a WARM welcome.

Two men might have engaged in a HOT argument; the verbal quarrel reminded them of the heat of physical combat.

The basic process throughout was: "this reminds me of..." When this thought occurred to ancient people, an old word got a new meaning.

This borrowing of physical words was not only for the purpose of expressing intangible thoughts; the process was also used frequently to name new physical objects that were somewhat related in appearance or function to the borrowed word. When tables were first made, a word was needed for the four vertical posts that held up the horizontal boards. These posts bore a certain resemblance to the legs that hold up and propel people and animals. Thus, tables have LEGS, and even a mountain has a FOOT.

The various parts of the body have frequently developed new meanings: the words HEAD, FOOT, EYES, HANDS, etc., are used in large numbers of borrowed senses. We speak of the HEAD of a nation, the HEAD of the class, the FOOT of a bed, the HANDS of a clock, the EYE of a needle.

Here are just a few examples of physical words that have been borrowed for use in other than their original sense:

BRILLIANT   The original meaning of this word is shining, as in a BRILLIANT star. Now we also use it in the sense of shining with intelligence, or smart. When we speak of a BRILLIANT idea, we do not mean that it literally gives off light, but that it figuratively illuminates the dark world of ignorance.

CHAIN   This word is used to indicate a succession of events that follow closely upon each other, or are dependent upon each other—much like the links of a CHAIN.

CIRCLE Your CIRCLE refers to your social or intellectual group; in other words, the people around you.

CLEAR/CLEAN Synonyms for these words have come to mean "innocent, morally pure." The opposite words— DIRTY, FILTHY—convey the idea of moral—as well as physical—uncleanliness.

CROOKED If you think of a *crooked* line, bending and curving every which way, and then think of a dishonest person, likewise evading and twisting the truth, you will readily see why CROOKED has come to mean dishonest. Similarly, the opposite word, STRAIGHT, means "honest."

EDIFYING An *edifice*, of course, is a building. From it was borrowed the word EDIFYING, which means "helpful to the *building* of brain and character."

FOXY This word means "clever" or "sly," that is, exhibiting the cleverness of a *fox*.

GRASP Originally, people *grasped* objects only physically; that is, they seized them with their hands. Now, the word means "to comprehend"—to seize with the mind.

HAUGHTY Coming from the French word for *high*, this word means "proud." A HAUGHTY person walks with his head *high*, and considers himself *above* others.

ROAD/WAY One literally walks down a ROAD or WAY, but one figuratively travels the ROAD to success or pursues a WAY of life.

SHARP/KEEN These words now mean intellectually SHARP; intellectually KEEN.

THRILL The original, physical sense of this word is now

obsolete. THRILL used to mean "to pierce, to bore a hole." Today, the meaning is preserved figuratively; to THRILL means "to affect emotionally," as if one's body were pierced by sensation.

TRANSGRESSION   Again, the physical sense of this word has been replaced by its figurative sense. Literally, *transgress* means "to go (*gress*) away from (*trans*) the right road." Figuratively, of course, to TRANSGRESS means "to sin."

Quiz 5

ARE YOU A GOOD WORD DETECTIVE?

Fill in the blanks with the proper figurative word.

1. The word for a program of studies comes from Latin *currere*, TO RUN, as though the _____ were a sort of educational racecourse.

2. A *repast* is a MEAL from Latin *pastus* (food). Cattle feed in the *pasture*. A man who gives spiritual food to his congregation is called a _____.

3. An *aura* is a BREATH, an EXHALATION, something you can almost feel. It is actually another form of the word _____.

4. *Feu* is French for FIRE. At a certain hour the call went forth, "cover the fire—go to sleep." This order was called _____.

5. When you feel a *bitter* taste on your tongue, it is as if something has _____ you.

6. *Brazen*-faced means IMPUDENT, as though the face were made of _____.

7. The *boundaries* of a country set the _____ for its authority.

8. When you follow a certain *routine*, you go in the same way, the same road, the same _____.

9. When you *count* up the money carefully—all that has come in and gone out—and give a report, we say that you are making an _____.

10. Latin *frag* or *frac* means TO BREAK, as in the words *fragments* and *fraction*. A breaking of the rules is called an _____.

Answers on page 180

Words Go Up and Down, and Fade Away

Words resemble people in many ways. There is a time and place when they come into the world. They live long and useful lives, working hard until, for some reason, they just die.

And like people, words often change their status; they go up and down on the social scale. We can call these, then, the elevator words—words that sometimes go up, but more often go down.

Outstanding among those words that have gone down in their social status are those that relate to country—as opposed to city—people. Countryfolk came off very badly compared to city dwellers. This was probably because the urban people set the literary language. Let us look at a sampling of words that have gone down in the social scale:

ARTIFICIAL   The Latin *ars* (skill) + *ficere* (to make) combined to form this word, which originally meant made by a craftsman. Its derogatory sense has emerged because of the contrast between ARTIFICIAL and natural. Nothing created by humans can surpass the beauty of nature. No matter how skillful the artisan, the ARTIFICIAL flower never looks so lovely nor smells so sweet as the real flower.

AWFUL   Used to mean full of *awe*, just as TERRIBLE used to mean full of *terror* and HORRIBLE, full of *horror*.

BOOR   Originally meaning "a farmer," BOOR has come to mean rude, uncultured, and discourteous.

CRAFTY   Although it used to mean "skillful," CRAFTY now means using one's skill in a somewhat sneaky way.

DOOM   Used to mean "judgment." We still use the verb form, as in "I DEEM (judge) it to be advisable." But judgments were so often adverse that the word has taken on its present meaning of an unhappy fate.

FABRICATE   From the Latin *fabrica* (an artisan's workshop), FABRICATE originally meant "to make or manufacture." The meaning has shifted so that FABRICATE now means to make up, or to lie.

FORGE   Like fabricate, the word *forge* really means "to make," as on a blacksmith's *forge*. FORGE has now come to mean, of course, to create falsely.

IDIOT   From the Greek *idios* (private), IDIOT used to mean a person who does not take public office, in other words, a *private* citizen.

JEST   Once meant "a brave and famous deed," but stories of deeds were accompanied by so much bragging and, perhaps, downright lying, that JEST now means simply a joke.

LEWD   Now means immoral or licentious. LEWD used to mean the *laity*.

RUSTIC   Literally means pertaining to the *country*, but the word implies the lack of the polish or finesse associated with the city dweller.

SAVAGE   Used to mean simply "living in the woods"; now SAVAGE means uncivilized.

STINK   Used to mean "smell." (A very lovely line by Chaucer reads "The rose stinks sweetly.") However, words that mean *smell* deteriorate. Instead of saying STINK, people began to use the word *smell*; now, even this word has gone down. When we say that something smells, we generally mean it smells bad. The word *odor* seems to be following the same pattern. When we say that something has an odor, we usually mean a *bad* odor.

SULLEN   Formerly described how a person who lives alone behaves; now SULLEN means unsociable or morose.

SURLY   Once meant acting like a *sir*, that is, a member of the nobility. Now, SURLY means rude or impertinent.

VILLAIN   Originally meant a worker on a *villa*, or farm. Hence, a VILLAIN came to mean a farmer or BOOR (see above), and finally took on the derogatory meaning of a blackguard.

VULGAR   Used to mean "of the people, the masses." (The great *Vulgate* translation of the Bible by St. Jerome was meant for all the people.) VULGAR now means coarse, unrefined.

Some words have traveled up the social scale. Below are some that have risen sharply in the course of the centuries.

CHANCELLOR   A CHANCELLOR used to be a clerk who

stood behind the *chancel*, the lattice that marked an office. A CHANCELLOR is now a very high official, either the head of a university or the head of a department of the government.

CONSTABLE   From the Latin *comes* (officer) and *stabul* (stable), CONSTABLE originally referred to the caretaker of the stable. It is now another word for policeman.

DEAN   From the Latin *decam* (ten), DEAN originally meant "a leader of ten people." Now, a DEAN is the head of a college.

KNIGHT   From the Old English *cniht* (boy), KNIGHT at one time meant just a servant. Today, the office confers nobility.

MARSHAL   A MARSHAL used to be one who took care of horses (*mearh* is Old English for "female horse"). Now, he has risen to head the entire army, or to be the one in charge of a parade or other function.

MINISTER   From the Latin *minor*, meaning "lesser," MINISTER originally meant "a lesser official," one who served the higher-ups. Now, of course, a MINISTER is a very high-ranking official.

PARADISE   From the Greek *paradeisos* (enclosed *park*), PARADISE at one time meant a *park*. Now PARADISE is a synonym for heaven.

PRECOCIOUS   Literally meant early (*pre*) cooked or ripened (*cocious*). It is now used in the sense of a PRECOCIOUS child—a youngster who displays the intelligence or maturity of an adult.

STEWARD   Used to mean "the guardian of the pigs" (from *sty*, the place where pigs are kept, and *ward*, meaning "keeper or guard"). Now, STEWARD is the title of a manager or supervisor of goods.

Words Just Fade Away—(Use old one)

Human beings have a tendency to boast. People exaggerate their achievements, even to the point of outright lying.

The fisherman returning from the day's sport, the hunter home from the hunt, the warrior back from the battlefield have all told tall tales about their prowess.

Because of this very human failing, people who listen to such stories will often discount automatically what they hear. They will reduce the report to something closer to reality. It is natural, therefore, that once-powerful words have lost a great deal of strength in the course of time. This phenomenon is known as *fading*; the word has become far weaker than it once was. The original force of the word has just faded away.

Here are some examples of faded words:

ASTOUND   Once meant to be struck by thunder; now ASTOUND just means to be amazed.

DETER   Once meant to terrify or to frighten away; now it just means to discourage or to prevent.

MORTIFY   From the Latin root *mors*, meaning to die or to kill, MORTIFY originally meant to kill. Now it means to humiliate or to vex deeply.

ORDEAL   Used to be some dreadful task—such as carrying

a red-hot iron or plunging a hand into boiling water—
that one had to perform to prove one's innocence. Now an
ORDEAL is just a trying or unpleasant experience.

STIGMA   Originally was a mark burned in the flesh. Now
a STIGMA is a much less physical and less severe mark of
disgrace.

THRALL   Is a very old literary word meaning slave. EN-
THRALLED once meant enslaved, but now it just means
deeply absorbed in.

TREMENDOUS   Once described something so dreadful
that it made people *tremble*; it filled them with terror.
Now TREMENDOUS means immense.

Quiz 6

ARE YOU A GOOD WORD DETECTIVE?

*Fill in the blanks with the proper "elevator" word or
definition.*

1. *Paternal* means fatherly; the *patron* is like the father in
   that he defends and helps one in time of trouble. The example of the father and the *patron* is one to follow and so
   the word for something serving as a model, a specimen,
   is _____.

2. The *roulette wheel* in the great gambling hall is always spinning, always _____ around.

3. *Rugs* are now made of wool or synthetic material; they got their name because they were originally made of tattered clothes or _____.

4. *Dorsal* means pertaining to the back. When you put your signature on the back of a check, this means that you accept responsibility, you _____ it.

5. *Flat* usually means level, smooth. When you continually give smooth compliments you are called a _____.

6. In days of old, an actor received his part written out on a *rolled*-up sheet of paper. His part therefore came to be called his _____.

7. *Plain* means clear, simple. The word that means to bring out the clarity or the simplicity of something, to clarify, is to _____.

8. *Lineage* tells of one's ancestry, of one's _____ of descent.

9. To *probe* means to search out the truth. To *probate* a will means to (the b has become a v) _____ that it is genuine.

10. *Wind* is air in motion, and some unexpected good things blown to you by the wind, that is, with no effort on your part, are called _____.

11. *Unsanitary* really means not healthy. There is another word like it that at one time also meant not healthy. It was a polite word for the mentally ill; the word is _____.

12. With a *ruler* we draw a straight line; the principles of conduct by which we live straight and honorable lives are called _____.

13. *Passé* (pronounced *passay*), a useful little word borrowed from the French, means that something is no longer in style: it has _____ its prime.

14. *Tradition* means handing over. The delivering, the handing over of a criminal from out (*ex* is out) of a country where he is hiding to the country that claims him is called _____.

Answers on page 180

Some Words Sound Alike but Don't Look Alike; Other Words Look Alike and Sound Alike

Throughout the centuries, the English language has received an enormous number of words from all ends of the earth. The flow of new words from many different sources is unceasing, even to the present day. It is only natural, therefore, that quite often words will have come to sound alike—and, as often, even look alike.

Homophones

The first similarity in words, and the easiest to learn and dismiss, is a similarity in the way they sound. We look at the words on the printed page and we pronounce them alike, even though they are spelled differently. For example:

The HEIR to the fortune.   The AIR we breath.

The AISLES in the auditorium.   The ISLES in the ocean.

The REED instrument.   To READ a book.

To SOW the seed.

To SEW the ripped dress.

The YOLK of an egg.

The YOKE of oxen.

To WAVE goodbye.

To WAIVE immunity.

The CARATS of a diamond.

The CARROTS we eat.

The CREAK of the stair.

The CREEK we swim in.

The mountain PEAK.

To PEEK at a picture.

The PIQUE he felt.

There are quite a number of these words. They do not represent a difficult problem because their meanings are so unrelated that you never confuse them in your speech, even when they are used together in one sentence:

He ATE EIGHT biscuits.

She was ALLOWED to read ALOUD.

Her BEAU wore a BOW tie.

He BLEW on the BLUE flame.

She ate CEREAL while reading a SERIAL.

YOU must shear the EWE.

We paid our FARE to the World's FAIR.

The BEAR would BARE his teeth as we approached.

Buying an expensive belt for his WAIST was a WASTE of money.

These words, which sound alike but have unrelated meanings and are spelled differently, are called *homo-*

phones. The word literally means "sounding the same" (*phone* = sound and *homo* = the same).

Homonyms

Now we come to a far more complex similarity—a similarity in spelling as well as in sound. These words are called *homonyms* (*hom* = same; *onym* = name). They are far more troublesome than the homophones, because they look and sound alike, but have different meanings and unrelated origins. For example:

> The BEAR was too heavy to BEAR.
>
> You CAN cut your finger on a tin CAN.
>
> She tried to HAIL a cab during a HAIL storm.
>
> Banging a tennis RACKET against a wall makes a terrific RACKET.
>
> He had to REST before he ate the REST of the pie.

Words have come into English from different languages, or from different dialects, or from different periods in the life of the same language; quite by accident some words have come to have exactly the same sound and spelling.

What do you make of these sentences?

> He is a MEAN person.
>
> The MEAN temperature was 74 degrees.
>
> Now this is what I really MEAN.

Remember that English descends from Anglo-Saxon, a Germanic language. From the German word *gemein* (a mean, common person), the prefix *ge* has been dropped, leaving our word MEAN, in the sense of "nasty."

The Latin word *median* (to be in the middle) passed through the French, and the hard middle *d* sound dropped out. Thus, *median* became our English word MEAN, or average, as in "MEAN temperature."

The Latin *men* means to be of a certain opinion or mind; from *men* come such words as MENTAL, REMIND, and, of course, MEAN, in the sense of "I MEAN."

Now look at these sentences:

> The laughter of little children has a lovely SOUND.
>
> He is safe and SOUND.
>
> Long Island SOUND is two miles wide.
>
> The ship's captain took SOUNDINGS.

The Latin *sonare*, meaning "a sound," became our English word SOUND, as in "the SOUND of laughter."

German *gesund* means healthy. (When you sneeze, someone will say "Gesundheit.") In old English, the prefix *ge* would frequently drop out. Thus arose our modern English word SOUND, meaning healthy.

The SOUND in Long Island SOUND comes from the Old English word *sund*, meaning "swimming." SOUND originally meant an easily swimmable—hence narrow—strip of water.

SOUND (to measure the depth of) comes from two Latin words: *sub*, meaning "under," and *undare*, meaning the waves. It literally means to go down deep into the water. When you SOUND out a person, you try to go deeply into his mind and thoughts.

Homonyms are also called *homographs* (*homo* = same;

graph = to write) because they are literally written the same.

English contains many homonyms. Below are some of the more interesting examples:

ARCH   (1) From a Greek word meaning the first or the most important, ARCH means chief, as in ARCH rival.

(2) The curved support structure called an ARCH was an important Roman contribution to architecture. The original word was *arc*, but the Latin *c* frequently softens to *ch*.

BALL   (1) BALL, the round object we play with, is related to BALLOON and BALLOT. (BALLOT was originally a little BALL crumpled up and thrown into a box).

(2) BALL, from the French *bal*, a dance, is an assembly for dancing, from which we have BALLET and BALLAD (a song to dance to).

CASE   (1) Coming from the Latin *capsa*, CASE means "a box." (A CAPSULE is a little box.) The word entered English through the French, which dropped the middle *p*.

(2) From the Latin *cadere* (to fall), CASE means "a special set of circumstances," or "the way things *fall*." (In CASE you are going to the store, please buy me a loaf of bread.) In this sense, the word CASE is related to CADENCE (the way the voice falls).

MEET   (1) To come upon (related to the word MEETING).

(2) Suitable; fit for (from the word *mete*, which means "measure").

PEN   (1) An enclosure for domestic animals.

(2) Quills were once used as writing instruments

or PENS. This PEN derives from *pena*, the Latin for "feather."

REPAIR   (1) From the Latin *re* (again) and *parare* (prepare), REPAIR literally means "to prepare again"; hence, to restore.

(2) From the Latin *re* (again) and *patria* (homeland), REPAIR literally means "to go back to one's country"; hence, to betake oneself; to go to habitually.

SEAL   (1) A large aquatic mammal.

(2) A device used to show that a document is genuine (from the Latin *signum*, a sign).

STILL   (1) In the sense of "stationary," the word STILL is related to STALL.

(2) The name for the apparatus used to make liquor, STILL, comes from the process by which it works—*distillation*.

WIND   (1) Air in motion.

(2) To move in a circular path (related to WEND, which means "to go around").

This pair of homonyms provides us with an example of two words spelled the same (and thus are homonyms) but pronounced differently.

Homogenes

Now we come to the group that is, in many ways, the most interesting of all—the homogenes. Like the homonyms that we've just looked at, homogenes are words that are spelled and usually pronounced alike, but have different meanings. There is, however, one tremendous difference between homonyms and homogenes: homonyms not only have different meanings, they also have different origins—

they go back to unrelated words. In the case of homogenes, however, the words ultimately go back—either directly or in some roundabout fashion—to the same word. Homogenes are literally words of the same kind (*homo* = same; *gene* = kind).

Let us look at some homogenes.

BOARD means:

    (1) A flat piece of wood;

    (2) To go on deck of a ship;

    (3) Food, as in room and board;

    (4) A group guiding a policy or company, as in board of directors.

At first glance, a board of directors has nothing to do with coming on board a ship or with the food included in the rent at a guest house. But these different boards are all related; ultimately, they all go back to a plank of wood.

The deck of a ship is made up of *boards* of wood. When you come on BOARD ship, you are stepping onto the planks of wood.

The table on which food is served is made of *boards*, and so the food itself came to be called BOARD.

The council of people who conduct the affairs of a corporation sit around a table made of *boards*. Hence, they are the BOARD of directors.

LITTER means:

    (1) Straw for bedding;

    (2) A portable couch;

    (3) Animal offspring born at the same time;

    (4) Rubbish.

The common ancestor of all these litters is the *bed*. At one time, the expression "making the bed" actually meant piling straw neatly together to form a place for sleeping. Thus, ancient beds were not much different, whether they were for people or for animals. Dogs and other animals would bear their young amid the straw that served as beds. And when the wind blew, what had been a bed could become rubbish strewn about on the streets.

There are a great many homogenes in English, and, in many ways, they are far more interesting than the homonyms. Homonyms came into English from different languages or from different dialects of the same language. But the story of the different—but related—lives of homogenes is locked up within the English language itself. The story of homogenes is the history of the language.

BAR You drink at the BAR; a lawyer is a member of the BAR; a BAR of gold is worth thousands of dollars; a guard will BAR you from entering an atomic laboratory. All these different meanings of the word BAR go back to the same stick or *bar*, of wood.

A *bar* of wood, propped up against a door, prevented people from getting into a room. This is the literal meaning of the phrase "BAR the door."

In the English courts, a *bar* was set up to separate the members of the court from the audience. Only the judge and the lawyers could stand behind the *bar*; all others were in front of the *bar*. Thus, a lawyer came to be called a member of the BAR, or BARRISTER.

Likewise, whiskey was kept securely behind a *bar* of wood, and so the place where you drink came to be called a BAR, and the man who gave you the whiskey became the BARTENDER. A BAR of gold has the same shape—but not the same value—as the original *bar* of wood.

BATTER We BATTER down a door; a cake is made from BATTER. In both cases, the original meaning of BATTER is to *beat*—the cake BATTER is *beaten* before it is baked.

BEAR We BEAR (carry) a burden; a woman BEARS (gives birth to) a child. The original meaning is to *carry*—befor giving birth, the woman *carries* the child in her uterus for nine months.

BOW We BOW our heads; an archer shoots with a BOW and arrow. Although the pronounciations differ, both words incorporate the original meaning to *bend*—the archer *bends* the BOW in order to shoot the arrow, just as the head *bends* down in prayer.

COACH The queen rode in the royal COACH; the voice COACH helped her to sing opera; the hockey COACH urged his team on to victory. All these COACHES originated with the verb to *carry*—the tutor or instructor *carries* you along in your work or sport, just as the royal COACH *carries* the queen.

CORDIAL We receive a CORDIAL welcome; we drink a CORDIAL. The common ancestor of both words is the Latin *cor* or "heart"—the CORDIAL (friendly) welcome comes from the *heart*, while the CORDIAL (LIQUEUR) warms the *heart*.

FALL FALL follows winter; the FALL injured the old man. Both words convey the idea of *dropping*—in the autumn, the leaves FALL from the trees.

LIKE/KIND   We LIKE people who are *like* us. We tend to be KIND to people who are our *kind*. It is human nature to be compatible with those who resemble us.

LONG   The bridge is a mile LONG; the prisoner LONGS for his freedom. The original meaning of both the adjective and the verb LONG is great *length*—it will be a LONG time before the prisoner's yearning is satisfied.

PORT   New York is a PORT; the skipper stood on the PORT side of the ship. The left side of a ship looking forward is called the PORT side because this was the side turned to the PORT, or harbor.

PREMISES   A no-trespassing sign was posted to keep intruders off the PREMISES; the two PREMISES led to a logical conclusion. The word PREMISE comes from the Latin *pre* (before) plus *mis* (from *mittere*, "to send"); hence, it means that which has been said or set down before.

But the word has developed in two different ways. Legal documents for the sale of property required a very exact description of the property. To avoid repetition of this lengthy description throughout the document, the word *premises* (meaning according to the aforesaid statement) was used repeatedly to indicate the property. PREMISES was used so frequently that it came to mean the property itself.

In logic, a PREMISE is a statement from which another follows logically. In other words, the premise is the statement *set down before* the conclusion.

TOAST   You drink a TOAST to the guest of honor; you eat TOAST for breakfast. A custom no longer in use gave TOAST its double meaning. Long ago, pieces of *toasted* bread were put into glasses of wine to enhance the flavor.

Quiz 7

ARE YOU A GOOD WORD DETECTIVE?

Fill in the blanks with the proper homonym, homophone, or homogene.

1. The girls spent the night in a _____. (hostile)

2. They began to _____ (martial) all their forces.

3. Character is written into one's _____. (jeans)

4. " _____ (flecks) your muscles," the trainer ordered the body-builder.

5. "There is no _____ (bomb) in Gilead!" cried the prophet.

6. "You are a lout and a _____ (nave)," he shouted.

7. A _____ (bolder) crashed down the mountain-side.

8. The donkey _____ (braid) all night.

9. The new television _____ (cereal) is on tonight.

Answers on page 181

Letter Changes Make New Words

Latin Hard C or K Became French CH

French often changed the hard *c* or *k* sound of Latin words to *ch*. This altered the sound of the word considerably and often made it difficult to recognize. For example, the Latin *camera* (room) became the French *chambre* and then the English CHAMBER.

As with many words absorbed into English from French, English retained the same word (*camera*) in its original Latin form. Thus, we again have a large series of doublets—words that originally were the same now existing in two different forms. For example, the Latin *sacellus* (a small bag) became our SATCHEL when the word passed through the French, but it also entered the English directly from the Latin in the form of SACK.

Below is a list of similar doublets that manifest:

(1) The original Latin with the hard *c* or *k* sound, and

(2) The *c* changed into the *ch* form of the French.

In all the cases below, it is easy to see the relationship between the two words:

Latin Form	French Form
CANAL	CHANNEL
CATTLE	CHATTEL
TRICKERY	TREACHERY
CANTOR	CHANT
BLEAK	BLEACH
BREAK	BREACH
MARKET	MERCHANDISE
CASTIGATE	CHASTISE
COOK	KITCHEN
BLANK	BLANCH
CANDLE	CHANDELIER
PACK, PACKAGE, PACKET	POUCH
COCK	CHICKEN
CARESS	CHERISH
CASTLE	CHATEAU
ARC	ARCH

Let us look more closely at some doublets:

CADENCE

CHANCE

CADENCE is a falling inflection of the voice; CHANCE is also the way things fall, or happen. Also related are the words CHUTE (a tunnel through which things slide down) and PARACHUTE (literally, "for the fall").

CAPTAIN

CHIEF

The Latin word for "head" is *caput,* from which we get CAPTAIN (the *head* person) and also CHIEF, via the French. The French form of *caput* has also yielded CHEF (the *head* of a kitchen); CHAPTER (a heading in a book); and ACHIEVE (to bring to a *head*).

CATHEDRAL

CHAIR

Here the French form is almost unrecognizable. CATHEDRAL is really a Greek word taken over into Latin, and originally it meant a seat (*cat* = down; *hedra* = to sit). The word was used to indicate the church at which the bishop had his *seat,* hence, an important, central, and beautiful church. The French changed the first *c* to *ch* and then, in addition, took out the whole inside of the word. What emerged was our word CHAIR.

CAVALIER

CHEVALIER

Both the Latin and French forms mean "horseman" or "gentleman." Also related is the word CHIVALRY, the code by which such gentlemen lived.

CIRCLE

SEARCH

In Latin, *circa* means CIRCLE, or going around. The French turned both the hard *c*'s into *ch*'s, producing the common French word *chercher* (to look around for). English changed *chercher* into SEARCH.

INCISION

CHISEL

From the Latin *cis* (to cut), we get the word INCISION. Passing through the French, *cis* became CHISEL, a *cutting* instrument.

PERSICO

PEACH

The Romans imported a new kind of fruit from Persia, which they called *persecum malum*, the Persian apple. The second part of the name was dropped, and *persecum* passed through the French. It underwent the familiar change from *k* to *ch*, and the middle of the word dropped out, becoming *pêche*. Thus, *persecum* became our familiar word PEACH. PERSICO is a *peach*-flavored liqueur.

L Became U

On the way into English, the *l* in Latin words frequently changed into *u*. This change was striking, and often made the word unrecognizable.

In Latin, *sal* is salt. The *l* is retained in SALAD and in SALARY (which was originally an allowance for *salt*). But the Latin *sal* also produced the words SAUCE (made with *salt*); SAUCER (a plate for the *sauce*); and SAUSAGE (meat prepared with a great deal of *salt*).

The Latin *sylvan* (referring to the woods) is evident in the word PENNSYLVANIA, or "Penn's woods." A SAVAGE is literally one who lives in the woods. The *l* first changed to *u* (*sauvage* in French), but the *u* dropped out in English.

The transformation of *castle* into CHATEAU involved the change from *l* to *u* as well as the change from *c* to *ch* discussed earlier.

A *calorie* is a unit of heat. With the transformation of *c* to *ch* as well as *l* to *u*, the Latin *calor* became the French word *chaud* (hot). Since the first automobiles had steam engines, the drivers came to be called CHAUFFEURS.

The Latin word *alb* (white) is evident in ALBUMEN (the *white* of the egg). It also inspired the name of the ALPS, high, snow-covered mountains. Another Latin word for white, *alburn*, passed through the French, undergoing the switch from *l* to *u*. The word was now pronounced AUBURN, but it sounded so much like BROWN that after a while AUBURN lost its connotation of whiteness and acquired the meaning of a shade of brown.

French G Became Germanic W

The Germanic and old Anglo-Saxon forms of many words began with a *w*; the same word in French was pronounced with a hard *g*.

Here are some of the doublets that incorporate the French *g* and the Germanic *w*:

GUARD, GUARDIAN	WARDEN
GUARANTEE	WARRANTY
GUERRILLA	WAR

Greek H Became Latin S

The Greek symbol for *h* often became an *s* in Latin. Since the friendly, impartial English language often borrowed both the Greek word and the corresponding Latin word, we have a series of doublets with essentially the same meaning. In the word roots below, the Greek form with the *h* intact is given first, and the Latin form with the altered *s* follows:

HALO

SAL

Both mean *salt*. A common word in chemistry is HALO-GEN (*salt*-making), which comes from the Greek. From the Latin comes SALARY, which used to be an allowance for *salt*.

HEL

SOL

Both the Greek and the Latin forms mean *sun*, as in HEL-IOTROPE (a plant that turns toward the *sun*) and SOLAR (of the *sun*).

HEMI

SEMI

Both forms mean *half*, as in HEMISPHERE and SEMICOLON.

HEPT

SEPT

The two forms mean *seven*, as in HEPTAGON and SEPTEM-BER (which used to be the *seventh* month, before July and August were added).

HERP

SERP

The meaning of these roots is *crawl*. HERPETOLOGY is the study of the life and habits of snakes, or SERPENTS.

HEX

SEX

Both these forms mean *six*, as in HEXAGONAL and SEXTET.

HOMO

SAME

These two forms mean *similar*, as in HOMOGENEOUS, AS-SIMILATE.

HYPER

SUPER

Both words mean "very," or "much of," as in HYPERCRIT-ICAL and HYPERSENSITIVE (from the Greek) and SUPERMAN (from the Latin).

HYPO

SUB

Both forms mean "under," as in HYPODERMIC (*under* the skin) and SUBMARINE (*under* the water).

The Letter N Moves Around

The letter *n* at the beginning of a word sometimes dances around, either dropping back to the previous word "a," making it "an," or moving from the "an" to the following word. For example,

A *napron*	is now	An APRON. (A NAPKIN is a small *napron*.)
A *nadder*	is now	An ADDER.
A *numpire*	is now	An UMPIRE.

A *naranj*	is now	An ORANGE.
An *Anne goat*	is now	A NANNY GOAT.
An *eke name* (*eke* means additional)	is now	A NICKNAME.

Quiz 8

ARE YOU A GOOD WORD DETECTIVE?

Fill in the blanks with the proper word created by a letter change.

1. A *bench* is a long, low seat. *Bench* also refers to the counter where money changers worked. The second meaning of *bench* inspired our word _____. (The "ch" has become a hard "c" sound.)

2. The festival meal was placed on a long *bench*. The word for the meal then became _____.

3. Another form of the word *car* and *carriage* is_____ (change hard "c" to "ch").

4. A *beaker* is a container for water. With a change of "b" to "p" and "c" to "ch," there emerged _____, another word for water vessel.

5. An *arched* passageway generally lined with shops is called an _____. (Here the "ch" is a hard "c.")

6. The bowman, one who shoots the arrow from the bow, (a curved instrument like an *arc*), is called an _____.

7. A *commodore* is a high naval officer ranking above a captain and below an admiral. An "n" has fallen out of the word. He really is a _____.

Answers on page 181

Prefixes Are Keys to Many Words

There are bits and pieces of words that can do magic—make words grow or even disappear; indeed, added to the beginning of a word, these bits change the face and meaning of the word forever. They are, of course, called *prefixes*. There are two important things to learn about prefixes. The first is simple and obvious: what does the prefix mean, and how does it affect the meaning of the word to which it is added?

In the following chapter, all the important prefixes, their meanings and usage, are discussed. Every prefix is the key to a great many words. Without a knowledge of the meaning of these little pieces of words, you are helpless; the task of mastering our strange and wonderful language would be impossible.

For instance, the prefix *ex* means "out"; anytime *ex* is added to a word, the word's meaning will change to incorporate the ideas of "out" or "former." *Trans* means "across," and every one of the nearly three hundred words containing *trans* conveys the idea of "across" plus the main part of the word.

The first step, therefore, is learning what the prefixes mean. This is simply a matter of memorization. The second thing to understand about the prefixes is a little more complicated, but just as important.

Let us return to the prefix *ex*, and see how it is used. The root *tract*, for example, means "to draw." EXTRACT would then mean "to draw out." The dentist will EXTRACT a hopelessly decayed tooth.

Now we come to our second principle in the use of prefixes and of the way they are attached to words. Human beings are lazy; they just don't like to exert themselves—or their throats. It is for this reason that people often change the form of a prefix just to make the word easier to pronounce.

Let us frame another word with *ex* and see what happens:

The root *ject* means "to throw." Suppose we want to say "throw out." The word should be "exject." But it is clumsy to say "exject," so people very sensibly changed the prefix by wrenching out the letter *x*. The word then became our familiar EJECT. If someone at a meeting is noisy and disruptive, the chairperson may very well request that the troublemaker be EJECTED.

Duc means "to lead." When we wish to speak of leading out or bringing out one's powers and capabilities, the word should be "exducate." But it is difficult to pronounce, so people simply say EDUCATE, dropping the *x* entirely.

Sometimes, a little more respectfully, the *x* is changed to the letter which follows it. "Exfect" becomes EFFECT, but since the *f* into which the *x* was changed is not pronounced, the EFFECT is really the same; it just adds a spelling problem.

Of course, what happens with *ex* also happens with several other prefixes. No matter how the prefix changes for the sake of pronunciation, the first two letters—or at least the first letter—are always a clear signal.

Let us look at how other prefixes change form:

Com means "together"; sometimes the *m* falls out, but the *co* always remains. Sometimes the *m* changes into the letter that follows. For example, to *labor* is to work, but "to work together" is not "comlaborate," but COLLABORATE. Likewise, before the letter *r*, the *com* changes to *cor*. We have CORRELATE (to bring into mutual relation), CORRO-BORATE, and CORRUPT. Quite often the *com* becomes *con*, as in CONVENE (to come together).

The prefix *in*, though very troublesome, is extremely important. To begin with, it has two completely different meanings: *in* means "in"; and *in* also means "not." This in itself is not so bad. You can usually tell from the way a word is used whether the prefix *in* means "in" or "not."

Often, though, there is a slight pronunciation difficulty in front of certain other letters. Whenever this occurs, the language forces the word to give way, making it change for the sake of smoothness.

For example, *luster* means "light." To bring light *in* should be "inlustrate." However, it is awkward to pronounce the *n*, so it was changed to a silent *l*. The resulting ILLUSTRATE is much easier to say than "inlustrate."

A person who is *not* religious should be called "inreli-gious." But again, the prefix changes and the word becomes IRRELIGIOUS. It is really not so hard to say "inreligious," but it's definitely easier to say IRRELIGIOUS. Similarly, something that is *not* possible is IMPOSSIBLE and not "inpossible."

Despite these changes in form, the important element—the letter *i* of the prefix—is always there, signaling that the prefix of the word is really *in*.

Another important prefix that frequently changes its last letter is *sub*, meaning "under." *Sub* can become *sup*. For example, the beams that carry (*port* means "carry") a building from *underneath* should be called the "subports," but you can feel the difficulty in pronunciation and understand why the word became SUPPORT. Similarly, we say SUPPRESS (to put *down* by force or authority) and SUPPOSE (to put *down* for consideration).

Sub can also become *suf*, as in SUFFER (to bear *under* a crushing burden) and SUFFUSE (to pour from *underneath*, hence, to spread throughout). Again the *su* of *sub* always signals the idea of under or beneath.

Ob means "toward, against." We change the *ob* to *op* in OPPOSE (to place *against*). *Ob* can become *of*, as in OFFER, or it can become *oc*, as in OCCUR, or, like the *x* of *ex* and the *m* of *com*, the *b* of *ob* can drop out entirely, as in OMIT. Nevertheless, the letter *o* always remains, indicating that the prefix is really *ob*.

The prefix *ad* means "to, toward, forward"—a simple concept that prefixes a great number of words. However, the *d* of *ad* is rather hard to combine with other sounds, and it changes in a bewildering number of ways. It can become *ac, af, al, ar, as,* or *at,* and even this is an incomplete list.

Here are a few examples of the *ad* prefix in its changed form: *ad* can become *al*, as in ALLURE (strongly attract *to*); *ad* can become *ar*, as in ARRIVE (to come *to*); *ad* can become *ac*, as in ACQUIRE (to obtain); *ad* can become *af*, as in AFFLU-ENT (flowing *toward;* hence, flowing with wealth).

Quiz 9

ARE YOU A GOOD
WORD DETECTIVE?

Fill in the blanks with the proper word or prefix.

1. *Supreme*, which means HIGHEST or BEST, uses the prefix
   _____, meaning *above*.

2. Latin *litera* means a LETTER of the alphabet. By adding the
   prefix for *not*, we get _____, a person who can
   neither read nor write.

3. RAIN in German is *regen* ("g" and "i" frequently
   interchange.) The process of artificially bringing water
   into the field (in a sense, bringing RAIN in) is called
   _____.

4. When you *commiserate* with someone you share his
   _____.

5. On the *contrary*, (as against this), contains the Latin prefix
   _____, which means _____.

6. They came to an *impasse*: their differences were so great
   they could not _____ through.

7. The word *leap*—"to jump, to go,"—has another form, *lope*. When a young couple runs off to get married we say they are _____.

8. An _____ jumps in where she's not wanted, or doesn't belong.

9. A word meaning DISTINGUISHED, MAGNIFICENT consists almost wholly of the Latin prefix for *above*. The word is

_____.

Answers on page 181

Important Prefixes Build the English Vocabulary

On the following pages is a list of common prefixes. As far as possible, they have been arranged in pairs, according to meaning. The purpose here is not to give strict dictionary definitions of the words that contain the various prefixes, but rather to show how the prefix works with the other elements of the word. We will see how the meaning of the prefix influences the meaning of the word.

These prefixes come largely from Latin, but some come from Greek and a few from Anglo-Saxon. We will start with the Latin prefixes:

Ex means OUT and *In* means IN

EX-PRESIDENT	The president who is currently *out* of office
EX LIBRIS	From *out* of the library of
EX OFFICIO	Coming *out* of one's office; hence, by virtue of one's office
EXPEL	To push *out* (*pel* = to push)
EXCAVATE	To hollow or dig *out* (*cave* = hollow)

The *x* of *ex* frequently drops out for ease of pronunciation:

EJECT	To throw *out*
EMIT	To send *out;* to send forth
EDICT	A speaking *out;* hence, an order proclaimed by authority
ELECT	To choose from *out* of a larger group

The opposite of *ex* (OUT) is *in* (IN, INTO, TOWARD):

INCISION	Cutting *into* (*cis* = to cut)
INCLINE	To lean *toward* (*cline* = to lean)
INCOME	Money coming *in*

Since the *n* sound in the middle of a word offers difficulty, the *n* of *in* is frequently changed to the following letter.

ILLUSTRATE	To bring light *into;* to explain, instead of "inlustrate"
IRRIGATE	To bring water *into*, instead of "inrigate"
IMMIGRATE	To go and settle *in* another country, instead of "inmigrate"

In sometimes takes the form *en*—ENLIVEN, ENLIGHTEN, ENDANGER, ENSLAVE, ENCAMP, etc.

In has a lengthened form *into* which means to THE INSIDE OF.

INTRODUCE	To bring *into* a society
INTROSPECTION	Looking *within* oneself

INTROVERT   One whose mind is turned *in* upon himself

Another form is *intra*, meaning WITHIN. For example:

INTRAMURAL   *Within* the walls of an institution

INTRASTATE   *Within* a state

Intra stands in opposition to *inter*, which means IN BE-
TWEEN; IN THE MIDST OF.

INTERSTATE   *Between* states

INTERJECTION   Breaking *into* the midst of

INTERPOSE   To place *between*

In also means NO or NOT:

INCAPABLE   Not able

INDELIBLE   *Cannot* be erased

INCOMMUNICADO   With no opportunity to communicate

INANIMATE   With *no* life

In (NOT) also changes for ease of pronunciation:

IRRELIGIOUS   *Not* religious

IMPOSSIBLE   *Not* possible

IMMEMORIAL   *Not* in memory; hence, ancient beyond all
                   memory

The *in* that means NOT frequently appears as *un*—UNCOVER, UNDAUNTED, UNDRESS.

Sub means BELOW and *Super* means ABOVE

SUBMARINE   Operating *under* the surface of the sea

SUBWAY   *Underground* train

SUBSCRIBE   To write (one's name) at the *bottom* of a document; hence, to show one's assent.

SUBTERRANEAN   *Below* ground (*terra* = earth)

SUBORDINATE   Of *lower* or inferior grade

For the sake of pronunciation, the *sub* will change form.

SUFFER   To bear up *under*, instead of "subfer"

SUFFUSE   To overspread with color, as though the color is poured in from *below*.

The opposite of *sub* is *super*, which means ABOVE or BEYOND.

SUPERHUMAN   *Beyond* human capacity

SUPERNATURAL   Going *beyond* the natural

SUPERLATIVE   Carried *above* all others (*lat* = carry); hence, surpassing all others

SUPREME   Highest; *above* all the rest

Super also appears in the form of *sur*.

SURMOUNT   To rise *above*

SURNAME	A name *beyond* the first name; hence, a family name
SURPASS	To go *beyond*
SURCHARGE	An excessive charge *beyond* the normal

Hypo means BENEATH and *Hyper* means ABOVE

This pair of prefixes is identical in meaning to the pair we just discussed—*sub* and *super*. *Hypo* and *hyper* come from the Greek. (Remember the Greek *h* frequently corresponds to the Latin *s*.)

HYPODERMIC	*Beneath* the skin (*derm* = skin)
HYPOTHESIS	A thesis or proposition set down *before* one
HYPERCRITICAL	Critical *beyond* all others; hence, excessively critical
HYPERSENSITIVE	Sensitive *beyond* all others; hence, excessively sensitive
HYPERBOLE	Thrown *beyond* the limits of truth (*ballein* = to throw); hence, an exaggerated statement

Ab means AWAY and *Ad* means TO, TOWARD, FORWARD

ABUSE	To use *away from* proper use; hence, to use wrongly
ABDUCT	To carry off; to lead *away*
ABNORMAL	Deviating *away* from the normal

ABRUPT   Broken sharply *away*

ABERRATION   A straying *away*

The *b* of *ab* drops out in:

AVERT   To turn *away from* (*vert* = to turn)

The opposite prefix *ad* is more difficult because of the *d*, which is frequently assimilated into the next letter.
    Here the *d* stays:

ADVENT   A coming *to* (*ven* = to come)

ADVERSE   Turning *toward* in enmity; hence, hostile, opposing

Here the *d* changes into the following letter:

AFFLUENT   Flowing *toward*

ACCORD   Turning one's heart *toward*; hence, agreement

AGGRAVATE   To add weight *to*; to add a burden *to* (*grave* = heavy, weighty)

ALLEGIANCE   The state of being bound *to* (*leg* = to bind, to tie); hence, the devotion or loyalty of a subject; the relation of a vassal to his liege lord.

Sometimes the *d* drops out entirely.

ASPIRE   To breathe *forward* (*spire* = to breathe); hence, to strive; to desire something above one

ASCEND   To climb *forward* (*scandere* = to climb);
                  hence, to come up

Pre means BEFORE and *Post* means AFTER

PRESIDE   To sit *before*

PREVENT   To come *before*; hence, to forestall, to
                  hinder

PRECEDE   To go *before*

PRECURSOR   One who runs *before* (*cur* = run)

PREFIX   Letters attached *before* the root word

PREAMBLE   Something that walks *before* (*amble* = to
                  walk); hence, a preliminary statement

PREFER   To set *before* the others in esteem

POSTPONE   To put off to a date *after* the original one;
                  hence, to delay. A person usually does not
                  set an earlier date, otherwise we would
                  have the word "prepone."

POSTSCRIPT   Something added to a letter *after* the sig-
                  nature

POSTHUMOUS   Born *after* the father's death; occurring
                  after one's death

PREPOSTEROUS   A charming word incorporating both *pre*
                  and *post*. It means "inverted; contrary to
                  nature," or "contrary to reason," as
                  though we were putting what should be
                  before, *after*—as though we made the *pre*
                  into *post*.

Ante means BEFORE

Another prefix meaning BEFORE is *ante*, as in:

ANTECHAMBER A room *before* the chief apartment

ANTECEDENT One thing coming *before* another

ANTEDILUVIAN *Before* the flood

Pro means FOR, BEFORE, IN FRONT OF
and *Contra* means AGAINST

When we refer to the "pros and cons," we mean the arguments FOR and AGAINST any proposition.

PRODUCE To lead or bring *forth*

PROCEDE To go *forward*; to come *forth*

PROMOTE To move *forward*; to advance in position

PROVOKE To call *forth* anger (*vok* = to call); hence, to incite or to irritate

PROLOGUE Words spoken *before* (*logos* = speech); hence, a preface to a discourse or a drama

PROGNOSIS Literally, to know *before* (*gnosis* = to know); hence, the forecast of the course of a disease

CONTRADICT To speak *against* or in opposition to

CONTRARY *Against*; opposed; opposite

CONTRAST Standing *against* (*stare* = standing); hence, opposition; divergence

Another form of *contra* is *counter*; indeed, to go *counter* is to go AGAINST.

COUNTERMAND   To issue a command *against* a previous command; hence, to revoke

COUNTERFEIT   To make *against* the truth; hence, to forge

Re means BACK, BACK TO, AGAIN

Here are just a few of the many hundreds of words prefixed with *re:*

RETURN   To turn *back*

RECALL   To call *back*

REJECT   To throw *back*

RECEDE   To go *back*

REMOVE   To move *back*; to take away

REPEL   To push *back*

RESPECT   Looking *back*; hence, regard; consideration; esteem

RESIST   To stand *back*; hence, to withstand; to stand up against

Com means TOGETHER, ALTOGETHER, COMPLETELY

The prefix *com* stays unchanged before vowels and before *b*, *p*, *m*. However, the *m* of *com* assimilates to many other letters for the sake of pronunciation.

COMPOSE   To put *together*

COMMISERATE	To feel pity; to share a person's miseries *together* with that person
COMMERCE	An exchange of merchandise; doing business *together*
COMPANION	One who shares his bread *together* with another (*pan* = bread); hence, comrade
COMPRESS	To press *together*
COMPEL	To push or force *together* (*pel* = to push)
COMPASSION	Feeling *together*; hence, fellow feeling in sorrow or trouble
COMPROMISE	To promise *together*; hence, a joint agreement; a promise to abide by a decision

Com frequently becomes *con:*

CONVENT	A company of religious women living *together*
CONCENTRATE	To bring *together* to a common center
CONCORD	Hearts coming *together* (*cord* = heart); hence, agreement
CONCUR	Fall *together*; coincide (*cur* = to run)
CONFLUENCE	A flowing *together*
CONGRESS	A group coming *together*

Before a vowel, the *m* usually drops out, leaving just *co* as the prefix:

COOPERATE	To work *together*

COEDUCATION | Boys and girls studying *together*

COGNATE | Descended *together* from a common ancestor (*gnatus* = born)

COVENANT | A coming *together* of minds (*ven* = to come); hence, a mutual agreement

The *m* of *com* is often assimilated into the first letter that follows the prefix:

COLLAPSE | To fall *together* (*lapse* = to slip, to fall); hence, to give way

COLLECT | To gather *together* (*lect* = to collect, to assemble)

CORRUPT | Broken up *altogether* (*rupt* = to break); hence, unsound; rotten

CORRODE | To wear away *completely*

De and Dis

De means DOWN FROM; AWAY FROM; REMOVING SOMETHING FROM. We have:

DEPOSE | To put *down from* office; to *remove*

DEPORT | To carry off or *away*; to comport

DEVIATE | To turn aside; to turn *away from*

DETRACT | To take or draw *away from* (*tract* = to draw)

DESTRUCTION | Pulling *down*; putting out of existence (*struct* = to build)

DECLINE	To bend or to go *down*; to turn aside (*cline* = to bend)
DETEST	To bear witness *away* from (*test* = witness); hence, to abhor; to dislike intensely
DECAY	To fall *away* in quality or quantity. Another form of this word is:
DECADENCE	To fall *away* (*cad* = to fall)

The prefix *de* may also mean THOROUGHLY, COMPLETELY, and have no other effect than to strengthen the verb:

DECLARE	To make clear (*clare* = clear)
DECLAIM	To speak or to utter aloud (*claim* = to cry out)

The other prefix of our pair, *dis*, also means APART, ASUNDER, SEPARATELY. In addition, it conveys THE LACK OF, or THE REVERSE. *Dis* is closely related to the prefix *de*. When the *dis* passed through the French, it lost its *s* and became *di*, or even *de*. Thus, the two prefixes have become interchangeable; the decision to use one in a given word depended almost entirely on pronunciation.

DISABLE	The *lack of* ability; hence, to make unable or incapable
DISAPPEAR	The *reverse* of appear; hence, to cease to be visible or present
DISAPPOINT	The *lack of* an appointment; hence, to frustrate an expectation
DISBURSE	The *lack of* purse; hence, to pay out

DISCLOSE	The *reverse* of close; hence, to uncover; to open up to others
DISSIMILAR	The *reverse* of similar; hence, unlike
DISCORD	*Lack of* harmony; *lack of* agreement

The *s* of *dis* often assimilates into the following *f:*

DIFFER	To spread or carry *apart*; hence, to be different
DIFFICULTY	The *reverse* of easy (*facil* = easy); hence, hard
DIFFIDENT	*Lack of* self-confidence; not believing in oneself (*fid* = to believe)

Per means THROUGH, THOROUGHLY

PERENNIAL	Lasting *throughout* the year (*annus* = year)
PERFECT	*Thoroughly* versed or trained (*facere* = to make, to do); faultless
PERFORATE	To make a hole *through* something
PERSIST	To stand *throughout* (*sist* = to stand); hence, to continue firmly in a state or in a condition

Per also means THOROUGHLY IN A NEGATIVE SENSE; COMPLETELY BAD OR EVIL:

PERFIDIOUS	*Bad* faith (*fid* = faith); hence, treacherous
PERJURE	To swear *evilly* (*jur* = to swear); hence, to bear false witness; to lie

PERISH   To go *bad* (*ir* = to go); hence, to come to a violent end

PERVERSE   To turn *bad* (*ver* = to turn); hence, contrary

Se means WITHOUT, APART FROM, AWAY

SECEDE   To go *apart from* (*ced* = to go)

SECLUDE   To shut off; to shut *away*

SEDUCE   To lead *away*; to lead astray

SECURE   Feeling no care; *away* from all care and worry; safe

SEDITION   Going *away from* (*it/ir* = to go); hence, revolt; inciting to rebellion. The word should be "se-ition." The *d* was thrown in to make it easier to pronounce.

Ob means TOWARD, AGAINST, IN THE WAY OF

OBJECTION   Something thrown *in the way of* one's path (*ject* = to throw); hence, an obstacle

OBSTRUCT   To block the way of; to build up *against* (*struct* = to build)

OBLIGE   To bind *against* (*ligar* = to bind); hence, to constrain

OBSTACLE   Something that stands *in the way* (*stare* = to stand)

OBDURATE   Hard *against* (*dur* = hard); hence, stubborn in resistance

Ob may become *oc*, *op*, or *of* for ease of pronunciation:

OCCUR

To run *against* (*cur* = to run); hence, to happen

OPPOSE

To put something *against* (*pose* = to put, to place); hence, to confront with objections

OPPRESS

To press hard *against*

OFFER

To carry *toward* someone (*fer* = to carry); hence, to tender for acceptance

OFFEND

To displease; to harm or to damage; to strike *against*

The following prefixes are fairly easy. Their forms hardly ever change, and they each have one simple meaning.

Semi means HALF

SEMICIRCLE

Half-circle

SEMIANNUAL

Half-yearly; hence, occurring every six months

SEMIWEEKLY

Half-weekly; hence, twice a week

SEMIDRY

Half-dry

Circum means AROUND

CIRCUMSCRIBE

To draw a line all *around*

CIRCUMFERENCE

The encompassing boundary of a circle; the line *around* a circle

CIRCUMLOCUTION

*Round*about speech

CIRCUMSPECT   Cautious; looking *around* (*spect* = to look)

CIRCUMSTANCES   That which stands *around* (*stance* = to stand); hence, the condition of affairs

Trans means ACROSS, BEYOND, OVER

TRANSPORT   To carry *across*

TRANSLATE   To carry *over* from one language to another

TRANSCEND   To rise above; to surpass; to climb *beyond* (*scandere* = to climb)

TRANSFER   To carry *over* (*fer* = to carry); to convey from one place to another

TRANSMIT   To send *across* space (*mit* = to send)

TRANSPLANT   To move *over* from one place to another

In a few words, the *ns* of *trans* has been dropped.

TRADITION   That which is handed *over* in belief and practice (*dar* = to hand over; to give)

TRAJECTORY   A throwing *across* (*ject* = to throw); hence, the path of a body moving by force; the path of a cannonball or a missile

Prefixes from Greek

The prefixes that come from Greek are used less frequently than those that come from Latin. Here are some of the more common Greek prefixes:

A or *An* means WITHOUT, NOT, LACK OF

The prefix *an* is, of course, related to the Latin *in* and to the English *um*, all of which convey a negative sense. We have:

ANARCHY — *Not* to rule (*arch* = to rule, to govern); hence, the absence of government

AGNOSTIC — One who does *not* know if God exists (*gnosis* = to know)

ANEMIA — A *lack of* blood (*haima* = blood)

ANESTHESIA — A *lack of* feeling or sensation (*aisthesis* = feeling)

AMORAL — *Lacking* in morals

Anti means AGAINST, OPPOSITE

ANTISLAVERY — *Against* slavery

ANTIDOTE — A substance taken *against* poison (*dotus* = that given)

ANTIPATHY — Feeling *against* (*patheia* = passion)

ANTISEPTIC — Something that works *against* germs (*sepsis* = putrefaction)

ANTIPODES — Places on the earth exactly *opposite* each other

Proto means FIRST

PROTOPLASM — *First* mold or form; hence, the life substance of the cell

PROTOTYPE	The *first* or most ancient type
PROTOZOA	*First* life (*zoa* = life); hence, animals of the most primitive kind
PROTAGONIST	The chief, the leading, the *first* person

Peri means ALL AROUND, ROUNDABOUT

PERIMETER	The circumference; the measurement *around* a circle (*meter* = measure)
PERISCOPE	Looking *around*; hence, an apparatus for viewing objects above the ordinary level of vision

Epi means OVER, CLOSE UP TO, IN ADDITION, ON

EPILOGUE	The conclusion of a literary piece, especially a play; *additional* words (*log* = speech or words)
EPIDEMIC	*Close up to* the people (*demos* = the people); hence, prevalent among people at a particular time
EPISCOPAL	Looking over the affairs of the church (*scope* = to look); hence, of a bishop
EPITAPH	An inscription *on* a tomb

Eu means GOOD

EULOGY	*Good* words (*log* = words or speech); hence, words spoken in praise of a person

EUPHONY — *Good* sound; the pleasing quality of sound

EUPHEMISM — A *favorable* expression substituted for an offensive one

Cata means DOWN, AGAINST, ENTIRELY

CATACLYSM — A washing *down*; hence, a deluge; a great upheaval

CATASTROPHE — A turning upside *down* (*strophe* = to turn); hence, a disastrous end

CATALOG — An *entire* collection (*legin* = to choose, to collect)

CATARRH — To flow *down* (*rhein* = to flow); hence, a runny nose

Anglo-Saxon Prefixes

Most of the Anglo-Saxon prefixes are clear and simple. There is no difficulty whatsoever in understanding what they mean and how they are used. For example:

After means AFTER, as in AFTERTHOUGHT and AFTERMATH.

All or *al* means ALL, as in ALMIGHTY and ALTOGETHER.

In means IN, as in INLAND.

Over means OVER, as in OVERTURN and OVERLOOK.

Under means UNDER, as in UNDERPASS and UNDERGO.

Out means OUT, as in OUTBREAK, OUTCRY, and OUTSIDE.

The prefix *a* means in or at as in ABED, ASHORE, AFIRE, ASLEEP.

The prefix *be* can imply intensive action, as in BELABOR and BEDECK. It can also convey the idea of taking away, as in BEHEAD.

The prefix *for* usually implies prohibition or rejection, as in FORBID, FOREGO, and FORGET. Sometimes, *for* means thoroughly, as in FORGIVE (to pardon; to give in *thoroughly*).

The prefix *mis* indicates that something is amiss; something has changed for the worse. For example, MISTAKE, MISLEAD, MISBELIEVE, MISDEED.

Quiz 10

ARE YOU A GOOD WORD DETECTIVE?

Fill in the blanks with the proper compound word or prefix.

1. The Greek word *dote* means TO GIVE. A substance GIVEN to a child who has swallowed poison, to work *against* its ill effects, is called an _____.

2. If you *judge* something *before* weighing the facts or listening to the evidence, you are guilty of _____.

3. The Latin *sper* means TO HOPE. If you are completely *away* from, or without, HOPE, you are in _____.

4. An *unruly* person does not follow the _____.

5. *Clemency* means GENTLENESS, MERCY. When the weather is threatening or harsh, it is _____.

6. When you say a man is *infallible,* you mean he can never

   _____.

7. The word *tail* means TO CUT. A *tailor* is really a *cutter.* In the past, merchants had to divide large barrels into small portions, cut large pieces of wood into smaller pieces, trim large bolts of cloth into pieces for individual dresses or suits. All these merchants, who *cut* and *recut* (*re* = again), were called _____.

8. *Guise* means a STYLE or FASHION. When you alter your clothing to hide your identity, you are _____ yourself.

9. A _____ is a reduction of the sum that you would normally pay. You simply *count off* (the prefix ____ means *off*) part of the money.

10. *Dia* means THROUGH, ACROSS. The line that goes *through* the circle, measuring the distance *across* is called the

    _____.

11. To *reveal* is to remove or to draw back the _____.

12. A wagon that *moves* by itself (*auto* = self), without the help of horses, is called an _____.

13. An invalid stricken by a *disease* definitely feels a lack of comfort, a lack of _____.

Answers on page 181

Suffixes Are Clues to Parts of Speech

Suffixes, unlike prefixes, have only a slight influence on the meaning of the word to which they are added. The prefix sets the word on the road it is to travel; the suffix just keeps it rolling along. Most of the time, the suffix will indicate simply that the word is a verb or a noun or an adjective or an adverb. Below are a few of the most important suffixes associated with each of the parts of speech:

Verb Suffixes

Ize means TO DO, TO MAKE. The name Louis *Pasteur*, for example, has been turned into the verb PASTEURIZE, which describes the process Pasteur invented. We also have:

HYPNOTIZE   To bring about a hypnotic state (Greek *hypnoun* = to put to sleep)

STERILIZE   To make sterile (Latin *sterilis* = barren)

ANESTHETIZE   To make numb

DRAMATIZE   To turn a story into a play

The suffix *fy* also means TO DO or TO MAKE, as in:

SATISFY   To cause satisfaction

JUSTIFY   To declare that something is just

SANCTIFY   To make holy (Latin *sanct* = holy)

VERIFY   To establish as true

The suffix *esce* has an interesting shade of meaning. It conveys the idea of BEGINNING or GROWING INTO. For example:

ADOLESCENT   Still *growing*, as opposed to an adult

EFFERVESCE   *Begin* to boil; to bubble (Latin *fervescere* = to begin to boil)

COALESCE   To *grow* together

Noun Suffixes

The noun suffixes usually mean the state, the condition, or the quality of. The important noun suffixes are: *hood, ness, age, ion, ism*. For example:

CHILDHOOD, BOYHOOD, ADULTHOOD

GOODNESS, KINDNESS, NEATNESS

SHORTAGE, VOYAGE, SABOTAGE

ADMISSION, DETENTION, PROTECTION

SOCIALISM, COMMUNISM, HYPNOTISM

A very important noun suffix is *er*, meaning THE AGENT; THE ONE WHO DOES, as in BAKER, BROKER, DEALER, and thousands more. The slightly unusual ending *ard* also means ONE WHO, but the meaning is always derogatory. For example:

COWARD	A timid, easily frightened person
SLUGGARD	A lazy person
BASTARD	An illegitimate child
WIZARD	A wise man who performs evil deeds
DRUNKARD	A person who habitually drinks too much liquor
LAGGARD	One who is always lagging behind

The noun suffix *th* is very old. Although *th* is no longer used to create new nouns, the words that have been made with this noun suffix are all important:

From *warm*, we have the noun WARMTH.

From *strong*, we have STRENGTH.

From *broad*, we have BREADTH.

From *dear*, we have DEARTH.

From *heal*, we have HEALTH.

From *true*, we have both TRUTH and TROTH (good faith; loyalty).

From *well*, we have WEALTH.

From *foul*, we have FILTH.

From *merry*, we have MIRTH.

From *steal*, we have STEALTH.

Adjective and Adverb Suffixes

Some adjective suffixes are *y*, *al*, *ic*, *able*:

HAPPY, RAINY, SULKY

NATURAL, NOCTURNAL, MATERNAL, PATERNAL

SCEPTIC, ASCETIC

CAPABLE, INFALLIBLE, IMPOSSIBLE

The chief adverbial ending is *ly*, as in BEAUTIFULLY and OCCASIONALLY.

Quiz 11

ARE YOU A GOOD WORD DETECTIVE?

Fill in the blanks with the proper word or suffix.

1. Unmarried women must have frequently worked at *spinning* for they were called _____. Some other words with the *ster* suffix (one who) are _____, a child, and _____, a criminal.

2. A *miser* is really a _____ sort of person.

3. The word *awful* now means BAD, TERRIBLE, but at one time it simply meant full of _____.

4. *Plumb* is Latin for LEAD. The repairperson who works a great deal with lead is called a _____.

5. A *liner* is a ship following a regular _____ of travel.

6. A person who is *querulous*— always peevish, always complaining—seems to be looking for a _____.

7. *Sloth* means LAZINESS, SLUGGISHNESS—a disinclination to work. If you put back the missing "w," you'll see *sloth* comes from the word _____.

8. A *locker* is a box with a _____.

9. *Breadth,* the measure from side to side of an object, tells us how _____ it is.

10. A *foundling,* a deserted infant whose parents are unknown, has been _____ by other people. Some other words with the suffix *ling* (one who) are _____, one who is very dear, and _____, an animal that is one year old.

Answers on page 181

Functional Change Increases Vocabulary

Functional change is actually a simple trick that allows the English language to increase its vocabulary greatly. It is a process that alters the purpose or use of a word.

Let us take, for example, the word *eye*. In its original form, it is a noun—a thing. But if a child's eyes follow a colorful mobile, the child is EYEING the mobile. We have now made the noun *eye* into a verb. A *hand* is a noun, but we can easily say, "HAND me the book," thus making *hand* into a verb. In the same way, one can THUMB a ride; FINGER the pages of a book; ELBOW one's way through a crowd; HEAD a committee; FOOT the bill; BACK a car into a garage.

Almost any noun can change its function as a noun and become a verb. And, of course, vice versa—almost any verb can become a noun. We speak of a great SHOW or a great HIT; we say it was a real FIND; it was a close SHAVE; a pleasant SMOKE. All these words were originally verbs that changed their function and became nouns.

Adjectives also change their function easily. Look at the word *better*. It is really an adjective, the comparative of the word "good." But we can easily say, "She BETTERED her position," and the adjective is now a verb. Indeed, we can also say, "He emulated his BETTERS," and the word becomes a noun.

A word such as *feature* exists as a noun (he had noble FEATURES); a verb (Paul Newman was FEATURED in the role); and an adjective (we enjoyed the FEATURE film). In the sentences below, the word *round* is used as a verb, an adverb, an adjective, and a noun:

1. Vasco da Gama was the first European to ROUND the Cape of Good Hope.

2. He went ROUND the mountain.

3. King Arthur's ROUND Table is famous in legend and history.

4. The father of the bride treated his friends to two ROUNDS of drinks.

English words can move with particular facility from one part of speech to the other—from one function to another—so that nouns can become verbs, verbs can become nouns, and adjectives can become both nouns and verbs. There is a complete merry-go-round of function in English words.

Sometimes when a word assumes a new function, purists get upset and protest the functional change. Ultimately, the protests are a little silly and totally futile; the process of functional change has been going on for centuries—for tens of thousands of English words.

Quiz 12

ARE YOU A GOOD WORD DETECTIVE?

Fill in the blanks with the proper functional word or definition.

1. The *fleet* of ships necessarily _____ on water.

2. *Vacant* means empty; a time that is empty, and free of regular work is called a _____.

3. *Luggage* is so called because we _____ it.

4. When something is *apparent* you mean that it _____ to be so.

5. The baby or the lion cub that *nuzzles* her mother is playfully rubbing _____ with her.

6. When you *imagine* something, you quite clearly see an _____ of it.

7. *Jam*, the sweetened boiled fruit that is spread on bread, is so called because it has been squeezed together, or _____ into a jar.

8. A *tumbler* is now a barrel-shaped glass with a flat bottom; but in days of old it was made so it could not stand upright: it actually _____.

9. The *duck* is so called because it often _____ into the water.

10. The *counter* in a store is now used for so many things, for example, displaying or examining merchandise, that its original purpose has been forgotten. Each store had a table or a flat surface that came to be called a *counter*, because on it the storekeeper would _____ the money.

Answers on page 182

Words Come from Superstitions

The fears of human beings range far and wide. Throughout the ages, they have shown that they can be afraid of anything in the heavens above or the earth below. They can believe almost anything.

A belief based on ignorance or an unreasoning fear of the unknown is called *superstition*. Superstitions have left many interesting traces on the English language.

Look at the expression "beware of the moon." In the Middle Ages, people were convinced the moon could cause insanity. If the light of the moon shone full upon a sleeping person, he would go mad. The Latin word for moon is *luna*; thus, a person with a deranged mind was called a LUNATIC.

The Four Humors

In ancient and even medieval times, people had a curious belief about the relationship between temperament and the physical body. This belief has generated many useful words, and it is important to understand it.

The body was thought to contain the four following liquids:

blood   (*sanguis* in Latin)

black bile   (*melan* in Latin)

yellow bile   (*choler* in Greek)

phlegm   (*phlegm* is a Greek word).

The ancients held that a person could be healthy and stable only when these four liquids were present in the body in the proper proportions. Since the Latin word for liquid is *humor,* a person whose liquids were in such equilibrium was said to be in good HUMOR. (*Humor* is also the origin of the English word HUMID, filled with moisture).

An excess of any of these liquids exercised a powerful influence on an individual's personality. An excess of blood made a man SANGUINE (from *sanguis*), that is, he was disposed to being hopeful or optimistic. An overabundance of black bile (*melan*) caused a melancholy disposition. A woman with too much yellow bile (*choler*) was CHOLERIC, that is irascible or easily angered. An excess of *phlegm* produced a PHLEGMATIC or sluggish nature.

The Latin verb *temperare* means "to combine in due proportion." So a person whose HUMORS were judiciously balanced was also said to be in good TEMPER. Her TEMPERAMENT was TEMPERATE.

Many such beliefs have given rise to common English words. For example:

ATLAS   From Greek mythology comes the story of a Titan named *Atlas* who fought against the gods. As punishment, he was forced to hold up the world on his shoulders. Atlas stood in an area in northwest Africa; the AT-

LAS mountains located there were named for him. The Titan's many daughters were water nymphs in the ocean nearby, and so the ocean came to be called ATLANTIC after Atlas's daughters. Since Atlas was often pictured with the world on his shoulders, his name came to describe any collection of maps. Today, the ATLAS is a standard reference work.

AUSPICIOUS   This lovely word conveys the idea that everything will turn out well. It comes from the Latin *avis* (bird) and *spec* (to look at). (*Avis* also is the root of AVIATOR and AVIATION, and *spec*, of SPECTACLE, INSPECT, PROSPECT, etc.) How do we go from bird-watching to a favorable sign? The explanation goes back to the augury of the ancient Romans. They looked at birds flying, singing, and crying in the sky to divine whether good or bad fortune was in store. The opposite word, INAUSPICIOUS, indicates that some evil is brewing.

CHIMERA   The Greeks believed in a fire-breathing monster, the *Chimera*, who had a lion's head, a goat's body, and a dragon's or a serpent's tail. Today, a CHIMERA has come to mean any horrible phantom that instills fear.

DISASTER   From *dis* (bad) and *aster* (star), DISASTER comes from a popular superstition of older times. The word means a sudden or great calamity, and it reflects the ancient, widespread belief that a person moving under the influence of a bad star would be unlucky.

The Hebrew phrase *Mazel Tov*, which is today translated as "good luck," originally meant "May all this take place under the influence of a good constellation of stars."

Many other words beside DISASTER come from *aster*. We have, for example, ASTRONOMY, the science that deals with the stars, and ASTROLOGY, a less scientific study of the stars based on the belief that they influence human affairs.

HYSTERIA   No man, according to the Greeks, can ever become HYSTERICAL. The ancients believed that this syndrome, which is characterized by wild screaming, was a disturbance of the womb. So they named it HYSTERIA, the Greek word for *womb*. Today, HYSTERIA is thought to be a disorder of the nervous system; it can afflict both sexes.

A HYSTERECTOMY is the surgical removal of a diseased uterus, or womb. The word has three elements: *hyster* (womb), *ec* (out) and *tomy* (to cut).

MALARIA   This unpleasant word is the name of a dangerous illness that produces a high fever. The word consists of two elements: *mal* (bad) and *aria* (air). The ancients believed that the bad air from swampy lands caused MALARIA fever. Of course, we know that the disease is transmitted by certain mosquitoes, but the name has stuck just the same.

Many words contain the root *mal*, meaning bad.

MALADY	Sickness; disease
MALICE	Ill will
MALEFACTOR	One who does evil (*fact* = to do)
MALEVOLENT	Showing ill will to
MALIGN	To speak ill of

PANIC   The Greeks believed in a god named *Pan*, who was

part man, part goat. The appearance of this creature—
or even his unseen presence—struck terror into the
hearts of all. From his name comes our word PANIC,
which means a sudden and extreme alarm.

How fertile was the imagination of the Greeks!

Quiz 13

ARE YOU A GOOD WORD DETECTIVE?

Fill in the blanks with the proper superstition-word.

1. A *ghastly* sight reminds us of a _____.

2. A *fantasy* is a delusion, a supposition that has no
   reality. It is a stronger form of a similar-sounding
   word, meaning a liking, or a _____.

3. One of the favorite superstitions of humankind is
   palmistry; a way of predicting the future by studying
   carefully the lines of the _____ of the hand.

4. *Morph* is a Greek word meaning FORM or SHAPE. *Amorphous* (a = not) means SHAPELESS. The Greek god of
   dreams and sleep was named *Morpheus, because he*

shaped and *formed* dreams. A drug that puts a person to sleep is called _____.

5. A *mystic,* with the help of knowledge hidden from all ordinary people, tries to come into direct communion with God. *Mystic,* then, comes from the usual word for a hidden or a secret thing, a _____.

6. People believed that in hell or the *infernal* regions, there raged a tremendous fire, called an _____.

7. Latin *dies* means day and *mal* means bad. If things are going badly on a particular day, if things look dull and gloomy, they are _____.

8. To *deem* used to mean TO THINK, TO GIVE JUDGMENT. The judgment must have frequently been dark, dreadful, and full of danger, because the noun born of *deem*, another word for the day of judgment, is the day of _____.

9. _____ is the mental power to see concealed things. It comes from the French words for *clear* (clair) and *see* (voir).

Answers on page 182

English Borrows
Words from Latin

The most important reason by far for the vast growth of the English language, from Anglo-Saxon times to the present day, is that English borrowed enormous numbers of words from many other languages. In particular, there were three great language treasure troves—Latin, French, and Greek.

The borrowing from these three storehouses continues to this day. Often, when a scientist or a scholar needs a name for a new development in science, technology, or thought, he finds a Latin or Greek term. The English language, in turn, has contributed generously to all other languages throughout the world.

The borrowing of English from Latin, French, and Greek accounts for more than half the words in our modern vocabulary. In this chapter, we will consider Latin as a source of borrowed English words. Chapters 17 and 18 will deal, respectively, with words of French and Greek origin.

In reading the following three chapters, please bear in mind that we will hardly be scratching the surface of this great linguistic movement—the flood of words pouring into English from Latin, French, and Greek. The words in these chapters are presented in family groups; that is, a Latin, French, or Greek root word will be grouped with several (by no means all!) of the English words deriving from it.

Four Major Periods of Borrowing from Latin

Latin is perhaps the greatest single source of English borrowed words, especially when we remember that many French words incorporated into the English language were derived from the Roman tongue. The infusion of Latin words into the English language has been a gradual process, with four major periods of Latin influence on English.

Latin words were adopted into the precursor of the English language by the Angles, Saxons, and Jutes even before they invaded England in the fifth century. For years, these Germanic tribes had been in contact with the Romans. This intercourse usually took the form of war or trade; hence, commercial words like CHEAP (L. *caupo*) and military words like CAMP (L. *campus*) were integrated into the Germanic dialects.

A more direct Latin influence on the English language occurred during the Roman occupation of Britain in the first century. Fewer than fifteen English words of Latin origin can be traced to this period, however, because the Germanic conquest of 449 A.D. all but wiped out the Latin vocabulary of the Romanized natives of the British Isles. We do know that the place-name CHESTER, which survives in such names as WINCHESTER, DORCHESTER, and MANCHESTER, originated during the occupation. CHESTER comes from the Latin word *castra* (a military fortification).

With the introduction of Christianity into England, in 597 A.D., by Roman missionaries, came a tremendous influx of Latin words into the English vocabulary. These borrowings include such theological terms as BISHOP, ALTAR, HYMN, CREED, MONK, PRIEST, and NUN. Since the clergy were among the primary teachers and educators in medieval England, we owe to Latin such words as SCHOOL, MASTER, EDUCATION, and LATIN.

During the English Renaissance, a rebirth of interest in classical literature and learning resulted in an enormous increase in English words of Latin origin. At that time, there was a concerted effort by writers to enrich the English vocabulary with Latin words, in order to "upgrade" the language. The learned words, or "inkhorn" words, as they were termed by opponents of this effort to "corrupt" the English language with foreign words, included FERTILE, CAPACITY, RELINQUISH, FRIVOLOUS, and COMPATIBLE.

English Word Families Based on Latin Root Words

AMARE   *To love*

AMATEUR   An AMATEUR acts simply out of *love*, and not for the sake of money. The word refers to someone who is not a professional, and, therefore, often denotes a lower level of skill.

AMIABLE   Used to mean *amorous*, or *loving*, but now AMIABLE means good-natured.

AMICABLE   Friendly; neighborly.

AMITY   Friendship; goodwill.

AQUA   *Water*

AQUEDUCT   A system of pipes through which *water* flows (*duc* = to lead).

AQUAMARINE   Blue-green color which resembles sea *water* (*mar* = sea).

AQUARIUM   A tank filled with *water*, in which fish are displayed.

AUDIRE   *To hear*

AUDIBLE   Capable of being *heard*.

AUDIENCE   A *hearing*; a body of people *listening* to a speaker.

AUDIT   To *listen in* on a course without taking examinations or getting credit for it.

OBEY   To *listen* to. From the Latin prefix *ob* (to, toward) plus *audere* (to listen), the word passed through the French, where it lost most of its syllables and became OBEY.

AUGERE
To increase, to enlarge, to put together
AUCTUM   *Having been increased*

AUCTION   A public sale. The AUCTIONEER tries to get *higher* and *higher* prices from the assembled buyers.

AUGMENT   To *increase*.

AUGUST   In a sense, *greater* than all the rest; majestic, venerable.

AUTHOR   One who *puts together* a book.

EKE   To *supplement*; to maintain; to achieve with effort.

BEN or BON   *Good, well*

A word of warning: A BONFIRE is *not* a *good fire*; it is a "fire of bones."

BENEDICTION   *Good* speak (*dict* = to speak); hence, a blessing.

BENEFACTOR   One who does *good* (*fact* = to do).

BENEFICIAL   Favorable to; *good* for.

BENEVOLENT   Disposed to doing *good*.

BENIGN   Kindly; *goodly*.

BONA FIDE   In *good* faith; hence, sincere.

BON BON   Candy. Literally, this word means "*good, good*," which is certainly descriptive!

BONANZA   *Good* luck; prosperity.

CANTARE   *To sing*

CANT   To speak in a whining, *sing-song* manner; the language of tramps, thieves, beggars; insincere speech.

CANTOR   Person who *sings* the service in a synagogue.

CHANT   To *sing*; a *song*.

CHARM   Originally meant an *incantation*. Now the noun CHARM means an amulet; and as a verb, CHARM means to attract; to fascinate.

ENCHANT   To come under the spell of; to bewitch.

INCANTATION   A formula of words *chanted* or recited in order to produce a magical effect.

INCENTIVE   That which sets the tune; hence, something that incites to action.

RECANT   To *sing* back (*re* = back); hence, to take back; to retract as erroneous.

COR   *Heart*

ACCORD   United *hearts*; hence, agreement.

CARDIAC   Of the *heart*.

CARDIOGRAPH   An instrument that monitors one's *heart-beat*.

CARDIOLOGIST   A medical specialist who deals with troubles of the *heart*.

CORDIAL   From the *heart*; hence, friendly.

CORE   *Heart*; central part.

CIVITAS   *City*

CITADEL   A fortress that commands a *city*.

CITIZEN   Originally, one who resides in a *city*; now, a resident of any community.

CIVIL   Like the residents of a *city*; hence, polite.

CIVILIAN   Now means any non-military person.

CIVILIZATION   The complex of human culture that developed once people began to live in *cities*.

CORPUS   *Body*

CORPORATION   A group organized as one *body* to carry out specific functions.

CORPS   A *body* of persons associated together; a portion of the army, forming a tactical unit.

CORPSE   The dead *body* of a person. Originally, the expression was "dead corpse" but the word "dead" was dropped.

CORPULENT   One with a lot of *body*; hence, fat.

CORPUS   The *body* of writings of one author.

CORPUSCLE   A living cell; a minute particle; any of various circumscribed *bodies* composed of many cells.

CRESCERE   *To grow*

ACCRETION   An *addition*.

ACCRUE   To be *added* to (*ac* = to).

CEREAL   Grain. This word actually comes from the name of the Latin goddess of agriculture, CERES, who was the deity who made things *grow*.

CREATE   To make; to produce; to cause to *grow*.

CRESCENT   The shape of the waxing (*increasing*) moon.

DECREASE   To *grow* less (*de* = away from).

DOCERE   *To teach*

DOCILE   Easily *teachable*; hence, tractable; obedient.

DOCTOR   Originally, a DOCTOR was a person who was so learned in the field of medicine that he *taught* it.

DOCUMENT   A paper that *teaches* or proves something.

LABOR   *Work*

COLLABORATE   To *work* together with (*com* = together).

ELABORATE   To *work* out in great detail and with great care.

LABORATORY   A large room where scientific *work* is carried out.

LIBER   *Book; bark of a tree*

The English word BOOK comes from the *beech* tree, the *bark* of which was commonly used as a writing material.

LIBEL   Slander. LIBEL literally means "a little *book*"; a long time ago, public scandal and defamation was spread by means of little *books*.

LIBRARY   A collection of *books*.

LIBRETTO   The script, or *book*, for an opera.

LOQUI   *To speak*

ELOQUENT   *Speaking* beautifully.

LOQUACIOUS   *Talkative.*

SOLILOQUY   Monologue; the act of *talking* to oneself (*sol* = alone).

VENTRILOQUISM   The act of *speaking* without moving the lips, as if the speech came from elsewhere.

MAR   *Sea*

MARINADE   *Brine* in which meat or fish is pickled.

MARINER   Sailor; *seaman*.

SUBMARINE   A vessel which can travel underneath the *sea* (*sub* = under).

POPULAS   *Citizens of the state*

PUBLIC   Pertaining to the *people* or to a community.

PUBLISH   To make known publicly; to issue copies of a book to the *people*.

POPULAR   Something that has found favor with the *people*.

POPULATION   The number of *people* living in a certain area.

REPUBLIC   A state in which the supreme powers of government reside in the *people*.

QUIES   *Quiet; to be free of disturbance to be calm and at rest*

ACQUIESCE   To remain *quiet*; to agree tacitly. Literally,

ACQUIESCE means "to give oneself" (*ad* = to).

ACQUIT   To be delivered; to be released; to be *freed* of all blame.

QUIESCENT   *Motionless*; at *rest*.

QUIT   *To be free of*; to be clear of. QUIT is really a shortened form of a word discussed above, ACQUIT.

REQUIEM   A mass for the departed; a prayer that eternal *rest* be granted. The prefix *re* acts as an intensifier to emphasize the idea of rest.

RIVUS   *River*

ARRIVE   To come to the shore from the *river*. Strictly speaking, of course, one could ARRIVE only by ship, but the word has become generalized and now applies to any means of transportation.

DERIVE   To originate; to be descended from. In other words, DERIVE means to flow from the same *river*.

RIVAL   Competitor. Originally, the word referred to persons who used the same *stream* and, as it happened, usually disputed the division of water rights. The derivation of the word is a rather sad commentary on human nature.

RIVIERA   The land along the *river* banks.

SAL   *Salt*

SALAD   Originally, a dish of *salted* vegetables.

SALARY   Money paid for services rendered. Originally, a sum of money was paid to soldiers to enable them to purchase *salt*.

SAUCE   A liquid accompaniment to solid food, often prepared with *salt* as a flavoring agent. (In French, the Latin *l* became a *u*).

SAUCER   Originally, a receptacle for *sauce*. Now, a SAUCER is a small shallow dish in which a cup is set.

SAUSAGE   Heavily *salted*, finely chopped meat encased in a cylindrical membrane.

SALVUS   *Entire; intact; in good health*

SALUTE   To greet; to wish someone *well*.

SALVATION   Saving the soul, that is, keeping the soul *intact*.

SAVE   To rescue; to preserve *intact*.

SENESCERE   *To grow old*

Implicit in many of the words that derive from this word is the idea that with age usually come experience and wisdom.

SENATE   A council, presumably composed of *old*, wise statesmen.

SENILE   Showing the characteristics of *old age*, especially associated with a loss of mental faculties.

SENIOR   One who is superior by reason of *age* or station.

SIRE   Male parent.

SIMILIS   *Like, same*

ASSEMBLE   To bring together at the *same* time.

ASSIMILATE   To be made *like*.

RESEMBLE   To be *like*. The prefix *re* intensifies the meaning of the root.

SIMILAR   Having *like* qualities.

SIMULATE   To assume—often falsely—the *appearance* of.

SIMULTANEOUS   Operating at the very *same* moment.

SOLE   *Alone, solitary*

DESOLATE   Left *alone*, deserted; lifeless. The word has come to mean without joy or comfort. The prefix *de* intensifies the meaning of the root.

ISOLATE   To place *alone*.

SOLILOQUIZE   To talk to oneself, that is, when one is *alone*.

SOLIPSISM   A theory, in logic, that the self can know nothing but itself *alone*; the philosophy of subjective idealism.

SONARE   *To make noise*

CONSONANT   (Adjective) in *harmony* with (*con* = together). (Noun) one of a certain class of speech *sounds*.

DISSONANT   Out of *harmony* with; discordant in *sound* (*dis* = apart).

RESOUND   To ring with *noise*. Again, the prefix *re* is intensive, indicating that there is a lot of *sound*.

SOUND   *Noise*; anything that can be *heard*. No one really knows where the *d* in the word came from!

TANGERE   *To touch*

TACTUS: Having been *touched*.

CONTACT   To *touch* mutually; to border on (*con* = together).

CONTAGIOUS   Something (usually a disease) that can be communicated to others by *touch* or other form of contact.

INTACT   *Untouched*; whole (*in* = not).

INTANGIBLE   Cannot be perceived by *touch* (*in* = not).

TACT   The word originally meant a sense of *touch*, but it came to mean a sensitive *touch* and, eventually, diplomacy; considerateness.

TEGERE   *To cover*

TECTUS   *Having been covered*

DETECT   To draw away the *cover* (*de* = away); hence, to discover the true character of something that has been hidden.

PROTECT   To put the *cover* in front of (*pro* = before), hence, to shelter or guard. Related to PROTECT is:

PROTÉGÉ   One who is under the *protection* of an influential person, usually for the purpose of furthering his career.

TOGA   An ancient Roman garment that *covered* the body.

TERRA *Land*

MEDITERRANEAN SEA   A large inland sea, so named by the ancient Romans because it was totally enclosed by *land* (southern Europe, western Asia, and northern Africa).

SUBTERRANEAN   Under the *earth* (*sub* = under).

TERRIER   A breed of dog. The TERRIER received his name because he would pursue his quarry into the *earth*.

TERRITORY   An area of *land*.

TESTIS *A witness*

DETEST   To bear *witness* against (*de* = against); hence, to denounce; to abhor.

INTESTATE   Dying without bearing *witness* as to one's wishes (*in* = not); hence, leaving no will at death.

PROTEST   To declare formally one's dissent; to declare solemnly, as if one were bearing *witness*.

TESTAMENT   The written record of a compact; evidence, *witness*; a will. The Old and the New TESTAMENTS were thus named because they provided *evidence* of the covenant between God and man.

TESTICLES   Male genital glands, which bear *witness* to the man's ability to father children.

TESTIFY   To bear *witness*.

TESTIMONY   Evidence given by a *witness*.

TEXTERE   *To weave*

In Latin textus means literary style—the way words and sentences are *woven* together. Thus the root *text* applies to words as well as cloth.

PRETEXT   Something *woven* in front of (*pre* = before), so as to conceal the truth; hence, pretense, excuse.

TEXT   The written or printed words and form of a literary work.

TEXTILE   *Woven* or knit cloth.

TEXTURE   The structure formed by the *interwoven* threads of a fabric.

UNDA   *Wave*

If you've ever sailed on the ocean, you've probably sensed its vastness. It often seems that there is nothing in the world of which there is a greater supply than the waves of the ocean.

Many words that derive from this root convey the sense of plentitude.

ABOUND   To be plentiful.

ABUNDANCE   A generous and overwhelming supply.

INUNDATE   To be covered with water. Literally, the *waves* are coming in on you (*in* = in).

REDUNDANT   Repetitious; characterized by using too many words to express an idea.

UTI   *To use*
USUS   *Having used*

ABUSE   To *use* something away from its proper nature (*ab* = away); hence, to mis-*use*.

PERUSE   To read or study thoroughly and carefully (*per* = thoroughly).

USURY   Originally meant interest, or money paid for the *use* of money. Now USURY means an excessive rate of interest.

UTENSILS   Domestic vessels or implements that have a particular *use*.

UTILIZE   To put to *use*.

VADERE   *To go*

EVADE   To *get* out of (*e, ex* = out); to avoid.

INVADE   To *go* into (*in* = in).

PERVADE   To *go* through completely (*pre* = through); hence, to spread throughout, to permeate.

VAGARE   *To wander*

VAGABOND, VAGRANT   One who *wanders* about, and has no fixed home. The word VAGABOND usually implies a carefree fondness for a roaming life. In contrast, the word VAGRANT implies disreputableness and the likelihood of becoming a public menace.

VAGARY   A fantastic notion that, in a sense, *wanders* about in one's mind.

VAGUE   Indefinite; imprecise; inconstant; uncertain.

VESTIRE   *To clothe*

DIVEST   To take the *clothing* away (*di* = away); to strip or undress; to dispossess.

INVEST   To envelop or cover completely; to *dress* in the symbols of office or honor; to commit money for a period of time in order to gain profit.

TRAVESTY   A ludicrous treatment of a serious work; a parody. The word literally means a disguise. A TRAVESTY is, in a sense, a literary disguise.

VEST   An article of *clothing*.

VESTMENT   Ceremonial *robe*; liturgical *garment*.

VESTRY   A room in a church where the vestments of the clergy are kept. VESTRY also refers to the group of people who ran the affairs of the church because they would meet in the vestry room.

VIVERE   *To live*

REVIVE   To bring back to *life* (*re* = back).

SURVIVE   Remain *alive; live* on; *outlive*.

VITAL   Pertaining to *life*; sustaining or central to *life*.

VITAMIN   Any of a group of certain food elements essential for *life*.

VIVACIOUS   Full of *life*; animated.

Quiz 14

ARE YOU A GOOD WORD DETECTIVE?

Fill in the blanks with the proper Latin-derived English word.

1. Latin *pati* means TO SUFFER, TO BEAR, TO ENDURE. The people who sit in the doctor's and dentist's office, waiting and suffering, are called _____.

2. An *incandescent* lamp is the same as a _____ in that they both give light.

3. The *Alps* are so-called because they are eternally white, snow-covered; the white of the egg is called *albumen*; a person or animal whose skin and hair lack colored pigment is called an _____ .

4. The Latin *ver* means TRULY—as in verily, verify. A jury, after listening to all the evidence, is asked to bring in the true judgment, or _____ .

5. *Lustre* is LIGHT. Pictures that throw light upon the events and incidents of a story are called _____ .

6. A Latin scribe would write with a sharp pointed instrument called a *stylus.* The way he wrote came to be called his literary _____ .

7. Latin *liber* means BOOK. The building where books are housed in large numbers is called a _____ .

Answers on page 182

English Borrows Words from French

The Norman Conquest of England, in 1066, resulted in a major upheaval of the English language. From the landing of William the Conqueror on English shores until the beginning of the thirteenth century, French was the official language of the English upper classes. French words gradually filtered into the vocabulary of the common people as well.

Not surprisingly, many of the French words incorporated into English during Frankish rule were political terms, such as GOVERNMENT, MINISTER, and PARLIAMENT. Many English military terms, for example, OFFICER, VESSEL, and SOLDIER, are also adaptations of French words, as are the legal terms JUSTICE, JURY, and COURT.

The French were the leaders in fashion in the Middle Ages, as they continue to be to a lesser extent today; hence, the words APPAREL, DRESS, and COSTUME were borrowed from the French tongue. In the field of art, the French have given us the words BEAUTY, COLOR, DESIGN, and ORNAMENT. Culinary terms of French origin include ROAST, TOAST, PASTRY, SAUSAGE, JELLY, and FEAST.

Initially, the dialect of French that was used in England was that of the Norman conquerors. In the middle of the twelfth century, however, the dialect of central France became predominant, in England as well as in France. Because of the differences in pronunciation of the two dialects, a particular French word often came into English in two different forms. For example, English took the words CATCH and WARDEN from Norman French as well as their Central dialect equivalents, CHASE and GUARDIAN. The Norman and Central derived terms came to have slightly different meanings in English.

English Word Families Based on French Root Words

BALLER   *To throw*

So many things get *thrown* about that *ballo* has branched out widely. In Spanish, the verb *bailar* means "to dance" (when you dance you *throw* your feet about). In English, the word *ball* means "an assembly for dancing," and *ballet* is a highly disciplined form of dance.

BALLISTA   In ancient warfare, the BALLISTA was a stone-*throwing* military engine.

BALLISTICS   The science of the motion of explosively *hurled* projectiles—such as bullets—from a gun.

EMBLEM   Originally meant inlaid work, that is, something *thrown* in or inserted. EMBLEM now means a visible sign of an idea; a symbol.

EMBOLISM   The obstruction of a blood vessel by something *thrown* into the bloodstream.

HYPERBOLE   Literally means something *thrown* high above (*hyper* = above); hence, an exaggerated statement.

PARABLE   A fictitious story used to teach a spiritual truth.

A PARABLE is *thrown* or set down beside you for your study and consideration.

PROBLEM Something *thrown* before you for solution (*pro* = before); hence, a difficult question.

CHAMP *Field*

CAMP A CAMP was first of all the *field* where the army might stay; the word implied that tents were put up to accommodate the soldiers.

CAMPAIGN From the word CAMP arose our word CAMPAIGN, which was first used for the army's operations in the *field*. The open *field* was a convenient place for men to go about slaughtering each other. The word CAMPAIGN then got to mean any organized plan of action, such as a political campaign—less bloody, but sometimes not much.

CHAMPION With the *k* = *ch* interchange, the CHAMPION was someone who showed his prowess in the camp, in the open *field* where warfare was carried on. The champion was often one who would fight on behalf of another.

CHAMPAGNE In France, a region of open, level country called *Champagne* produces the bubbly wine that we call CHAMPAGNE.

CHASE *To pursue*

The Latin word *capt* means to take, to capture; with our familiar *k* = *ch* interchange, came the Old French word *chacier*, which in English became chase.

CHASE   To follow, usually rapidly and purposefully, with the intention of overtaking, arresting, or doing violence to someone or something.

CATCH   To CATCH is a form of to capture, and then it also came to mean CHASE for the purpose of acquiring, of capturing.

PURCHASE   A variation of the word CATCH. The prefix *pur* could mean thoroughly. Today, it simply means to put money down and receive an item. But the word has a much more violent image in it. It means to go chasing after something with passion.

A department store in Boston, Filene's, sells extremely expensive designer clothing at very low prices. At the sound of the 9:30 opening bell, hordes of Boston women, their eyes alight, go for the dresses like hunters after prey. Here we see the word purchase—to chase thoroughly after something—come alive.

CHEF   *Head*

Latin *caput* means HEAD; with the *k* = *ch* interchange came the French CHEF.

CHIEF   A person in charge.

CHEF   Cook. This usage might be a little more puzzling; but of course a CHEF is not an ordinary cook. He is the *chief* cook, the head of all; in his own way, an artist of distinction.

KERCHIEF   A cover for the *head*. Handkerchief really means a small kerchief.

ACHIEVE   To finish, to accomplish; actually to bring to a desired result.

MISCHIEF   Misfortune, distress, harm or injury. MISCHIEF literally means coming to a *head*, or a bad end. (*mis* = bad).

FACE   *To front, to comfort*

DEFACE   To mar the appearance of, to blot out, to remove, or to alter the *face* (*de* = away).

EFFACE   To wipe out, to obliterate. The prefix is really *ex*, which means "out."

FACETS   Sides or *faces*. A diamond can have many FACETS —really many *faces*—and so can a problem or a question.

SURFACE   The outermost part of any material body; literally, on the *face* of. The prefix *super*—above—has become *sur* in French. SURFACE is the same as SUPERFICIAL, which also means on the surface or on the face of.

FACADE   The principal front of the building—its *face*.

FILE   *A string or wire*

FILE   A FILE was originally a *string* or *wire* on which papers were strung and arranged carefully in order. From this simple.*wire* came the complicated filing systems of today.

FILAMENT   A tenuous, *wire-like* body. The most common FILAMENT is that in the electic bulb.

FILIGREE   Ornamental work of fine *wire*. In the Orient, exquisite FILIGREE jewelry is made with fine metal threads.

FILET   A strip or slice of fish or meat without bones. The British spell FILET with two *l*'s.

DEFILE   A narrow pass between mountains. In the past, soldiers would march through such a pass in single file, their column stretching out like a long *wire*. DEFILE came to mean the pass itself.

   Be careful: There is another DEFILE, a homograph— remember the chapter on homographs, homophones, homogenes. This DEFILE means "making foul or unclean."

GRAVE   *Heavy*

AGGRAVATE   To make *heavier* and more burdensome; hence, to add to one's troubles.

GRAVE   Important; weighty; serious.

GRAVITY   The attraction of weight.

GRIEF   *Heavy* with sorrow; hence, emotional suffering.

JOUR   *Day*

This French word comes from the Latin *diurnis* (daily).

ADJOURN   To finish the matters belonging to the *day*; hence, to suspend.

JOURNAL   A written account of all the events of the *day*.

JOURNEY   A trip. Although today the word JOURNEY can mean a trip of any duration, at one time a JOURNEY referred only to a trip lasting exactly one *day*.

JOURNEYMAN   One who works by the *day*.

LIMES   *Boundary, threshold*

ELIMINATE   To throw out the doorway or across the *threshold;* hence, to remove (*e, ex* = out).

LIMIT   The outer extent of an area. The *threshold* is, of course, the outer extent of a house.

PRELIMINARY   In front of the *threshold;* hence, whatever comes before the main action (*pre* = before).

MIRACULEUX   *Wonderful*

ADMIRE   Originally meant to *wonder* at; to be astonished. The meaning has changed slightly in time, so that today, ADMIRE means to esteem; to regard highly.

MARVEL   To *wonder* at.

MIRACLE   Something to *wonder* at.

MORT   *Death*

The great, central, inescapable fact of life is the presence, the certainty, the inevitable coming of death. There has always been a passionate hope and belief that somehow death is not the end, that we shall become IMMORTAL, that is, that the soul will live on in some future. But because we must die, the word MORTAL has come to mean a human being. Socrates put it very succinctly when he said that all men are MORTAL, Socrates is a man, therefore Socrates is MORTAL.

MORIBUND   Coming to an end, about to die.

AMORTIZE   To kill a debt, to pay it off gradualy.

MURDER   To kill, to cause to *die*.

POST MORTEM   An examination of a corpse to determine the cause of *death*.

MORTUARY   A place for the temporary reception of the *dead*.

MORTIFY   Now means to humiliate, to cause a severe wound to someone's pride or self complacency. But the original meaning was much stronger—to kill.

OPTIQUE   *Pertaining to sight or to the eye*

AUTOPSY   A post-mortem examination of a body. Since *auto* means "oneself" and *opsy* means "to see," the word literally means *to see* for oneself what actually happened to cause death.

BIOPSY   The removal of tissue from the body for examination. BIOPSY literally means *to look at* living tissue (*bio* = living).

OPTICIAN   A person who makes or sells instruments that have to do with *sight*.

OPTICS   The science dealing with *sight*.

PAIR   *Two of a kind, usually the same*

PEER   A member of the nobility—one who has equal rank with you; that is, of course, if you are a member of the nobility. But today, it is used for anyone who is equal to you.

PEERLESS   Having no PEER, no equal; matchless.

DISPARITY   Inequality, unlikeness.

DISPARAGE   Used to mean to match unequally—usually by marrying someone not equal to you in rank. Now, of course, it means to speak slightingly of. It is not entirely clear how the present meaning developed.

COMPARE   To represent something as being similar to something else.

POSER   *To place*

POSITION   Where someone or something has been *placed*.

POSE   A position, an attitude that you assume. Models *pose* for artists.

EXPOSITION   A public *display* of new artistic, industrial, and scientific products.

EXPOSE   To lay open, to disclose, to exhibit.

COMPOSE   To put together—*com* means together. Words or music can be put together—composed. COMPOSE can also mean to put together troubled thoughts or feelings in a happy way. When someone is angry or upset, we say to him, "COMPOSE yourself."

PROPOSAL   A *plan* put before someone. This *plan* could be an offer of marriage.

DEPOSIT   To put down or into. A DEPOSIT usually means the *placing* of money into a bank.

ROLLE   *A little wheel*

ROLL   A piece of parchment made into a cylindrical form.

All important documents and records of monies owed, or property owned, were written on ROLLS. These documents were written in duplicate, and kept in a central place in a government office. They were called the COUNTER ROLLS; that is, the ROLLS that correspond to the originals.

The government official in charge of these COUNTER ROLLS, a person of great power and authority, came to be called the CONTROLLER. This word is sometimes spelled *comptroller*.

Of course, the most popular use of ROLL today is the round piece of bread for sandwiches.

ROLE   The actor's part was given to him on a parchment ROLL, and the word came to be spelled ROLE.

ROTUND   Round, rounded.

SAUF   *Safe, well*

SALVATION   Coming into a state of *well-being*.

SALUTE   To greet. We SALUTE those whom we wish *well*.

SALVER   In the Middle Ages poisoning food was a very common and convenient way of disposing of enemies. Every castle had a man called the SALVER who tasted all the food; and if it was poisoned, he died, and the rest were SAVED. But the French dropped the *l* and the word became our very common word SAFE—free from hurt, damage, or danger.

SAFE   As a noun, of course, a SAFE is for the safekeeping of valuables.

SAVIOR   The Redeemer, the one who will SAVE humanity.

Quiz 15

ARE YOU A GOOD WORD DETECTIVE?

Fill in the blanks with the proper French-derived English word.

1. The servant who carries the *bottle* of wine to the table is called the _____.

2. When you want to make *sure* that you do not suffer a great loss from fire or theft, you take out _____.

3. French *parler* means TO SPEAK; the room in the house where we sit and talk is called the _____.

4. A *coroner* is a public official whose chief duty is to investigate deaths that are believed to have stemmed from unnatural causes. In the days when most countries were ruled by kings, this official was called a *coroner* because he was an officer of the _____.

5. *Malaise* means BODILY DISCOMFORT or SUFFERING. The prefix is *mal* (bad) and the suffix is our common word *ease*. We use a similar word for illness, with the prefix *dis* (bad). This is the familiar word _____.

6. When you keep an appointment with a friend, *rendering* yourself to a specific place at a specific time, you are keeping a _____.

Answers on page 182

English Borrows
Words from Greek

Greek and Latin are really sister languages; both descended from the ancient Indo-European parent language. Thus, many words in these two languages may ultimately derive from the same, very ancient root. This root may also have come down to such disparate peoples as the Hindus of India, the Persians of Iran, and the great Germanic tribes, since they all descended from the primitive Indo-European tribes of southeastern Europe.

While fewer Greek words have been adopted into the English language than Latin or French words, Greek has had an appreciable indirect influence on our language. This indirect influence came about because English has borrowed extensively from Latin, which in turn had earlier borrowed many words from Greek.

Why did the Latin language borrow so heavily from its sister language? Let us look back at history. Greek culture—which produced so many great philosophers, playwrights, poets, and sculptors—was the flower of ancient civilization. But the Romans, who possessed superior military genius and organization, easily conquered the small, disunited Greek city-states. The Romans were quick to appreciate the great beauty and vitality of Greek drama, Greek poetry, Greek philosophy. Although Rome had conquered Greece in the military sense, the Greeks made an absolute cultural conquest of the Romans.

Along with the culture of the Greeks, of course, went their language. A Greek slave who could teach his language to Roman children was worth a fortune. A huge number of Greek words poured in a steady stream into the Latin language. Thus, when we trace a word back to Latin, it could very easily have been a Greek word originally. The words CLIMAX, CHAOS, and ENTHUSIASM were all acquired by Latin from Greek.

The greatest period of direct Greek influence on English was the sixteenth century. The revived study of Greek during the Renaissance caused such words as CATASTROPHE, DEMOCRACY, ENCYCLOPEDIA, AUTOGRAPH, HALO, and BENEFIT to be introduced into our language.

Before this influx of Greek words during the Renaissance, the primary Greek influence on English vocabulary had been in supplying scientific words. Today, we continue to borrow scientific and technical terms from the Greeks; we have given Greek names to many modern inventions, such as the TELEPHONE and the STETHOSCOPE, and to processes undreamed of by the ancients, such as PHOTOGRAPHY and LITHOGRAPHY.

English Word Families Based on Greek Root Words

AGEIN   *To lead; to drive*

AGONY   This word reflects a curious turn taken by the root *ago*. It came to mean a gathering for sports, then it became an athletic contest, and finally the word AGONY was applied to the effort involved in the athletic contest. AGONY now means anguish of mind or extreme bodily suffering.

ANTAGONIST   One who *drives* against you (*anti* = against); hence, opponent.

DEMAGOGUE   One who *leads* the people (*demo* = people). This is a derogatory word, usually applied to a leader who is interested only in his own power and wealth.

PEDAGOGUE   One who *leads* the young; hence, a teacher.

PROTAGONIST   One who takes the *leading* role in a contest or play (*proto* = first).

SYNAGOGUE   A congregation of Jews gathered for worship (*syn* = together). Also, the actual building of assembly used for worship. The great Christian scholar Travers Hereford said, "The Jews have scarcely done anything more wonderful in their long history than to create the synagogue," which provided the model for the organization of both the Christian church and the Moslem mosque.

AMPHI—AMBI   *On both sides; all around*

AMBIDEXTROUS   This word refers to a person who can use *both* hands equally well. The word *dexter* means right-handed; the implication is that the person has two right hands.

AMBIGUOUS   Having *two* or more meanings.

AMBIVALENT   Having opposite or conflicting opinions at the same time.

AMPHIBIOUS   Able to live *both* in water and on land (*bio* = live).

AMPHITHEATER   An oval or circular building built *around* an arena.

ANTHROPOS *Man*

ANTHROPOLOGY   The study of the races and the development of *man* (*ology* = the study of).

ANTHROPOMORPHISM   Ascribing the *human* form to a deity.

MISANTHROPIST   One who hates his fellow *man* (*mis* = to hate).

PHILANTHROPIST   One who loves his fellow *man* (*phil* = to love).

AUTO *Self*

AUTOBIOGRAPHY   The story of a person's life written by the person *himself* (*bio* = life).

AUTOCRAT   Absolute ruler; one who rules all by *himself*.

AUTOGRAPH   Your signature written by *yourself* (*graph* = to write.

AUTOMOBILE   To move *oneself* (*mobile* = to move); motor car.

AUTONOMY   *Self-rule* by a group (*nomos* = rule, law).

BARUS *Heavy*

BARITONE   A singer who has a *heavy* or a deep voice (*tone* = voice).

BARIUM   A *heavy* element.

BAROMETER   An instrument that measures how *heavy* the atmosphere is (*meter* = to measure).

BIOS *Life*

ANTIBIOTIC   Literally means against *life* (*anti* = against), but this drug works against the life of bacteria, the microscopic organisms that threaten human life. Thus, an ANTIBIOTIC is actually supportive of the *life* that really counts—human life.

BIOCHEMISTRY   The branch of chemistry that deals with plant and animal *life*.

BIOGRAPHY   The written story of a person's *life* (*graph* = writing).

BIOLOGY   The study of *life* (*ology* = the study of).

MICROBIOLOGY   The branch of biology that deals with minute *life* forms (*micro* = small).

DEMOS *People*

DEMAGOGUE   A leader of the *people*. Used in a derogatory sense. See AGEIN.

DEMOCRACY   Rule by the *people* (*kratos* = rule, power).

EPIDEMIC   A disease that is widespread among the *people* (*epi* = close up to).

DYNAMOS   *Strength, power*

DYNAMIC   Characterized by energy or *power*.

DYNAMITE   A *powerful* explosive.

DYNAMO   A machine that generates electric *power*.

DYNASTY   A succession of rulers of the same line of descent. The rulers, of course, exercise their *power* to rule.

DINOSAUR   A large, extinct reptile characterized by great and fearsome *strength*.

EDOS   *Form*

ANTHROPOID   Having the *form* of man (*anthropos* = man). See ANTHROPOS.

IDOL   A visible *form*; an image.

SPHEROID   Having the *form* of a sphere.

GNOSIS   *To know*

According to Grimm's Law, the hard *g* becomes *k*; hence, the word KNOW comes directly from *gnosis*. The changeover looks a little strange to us today only because we no longer pronounce the *k* sound.

AGNOSTIC   One who does not *know* whether God exists (*a* = not).

DIAGNOSIS   Literally, to *know* thoroughly (*dia* = thoroughly); hence, a determination of the nature of a disease.

GNOSTIC   A member of an ancient religious sect. The GNOSTICS believed they had a unique *knowledge* of the mysteries of life.

PROGNOSIS   *Know* before (*pro* = before); hence, a forecast of the course a disease will take.

HODOS   *Way; journey*

Because the initial letter *h* has a very weak sound, it frequently dies out.

EPISODE   An incident in the course of events in a person's life or experience. Literally, an EPISODE comes in along the *way*.

EXODUS   Mass departure; *journey* out (*ex* = out).

METHOD   A systematic *way* of doing something.

HOMOLOS   *Same, uniform*

HOMOGENIZED   Blended so thoroughly as to achieve unvarying *uniformity*.

HOMONYM   One of two words that have the *same* name but different meanings (*nym* = name).

HOMOSEXUAL   One who has sexual feelings for a person of the *same* sex.

HYDOR   *Water*

HYDRA   A *water* snake of Greek legend that grew two heads when one was cut off.

HYDRANT A pipe from which *water* is drawn to fight fires.

HYDROPHOBIA A convulsive fear of *water* (*phobia* = fear of); rabies.

KALOS *Beautiful*

CALLIGRAPHY *Beautiful* writing (*graph* = writing).

CALISTHENICS Bodily exercise to promote health, grace, and *beauty* (*sthenos* = strength).

CALLIPYGIAN There is a proverb that says "the Greek had a word for it." One word they had is CALLIPYGIAN: it means having *beautiful* buttocks.

KALEIDOSCOPE An instrument through which one sees *beautiful* shapes (*scope* = to see; *eid* = forms, shapes).

KRUPTOS *Hidden, secret*

APOCRYPHA The books that were excluded from the canon of the Bible. These writings were *hidden* away from the people.

CRYPT An underground or *hidden* chamber.

CRYPTIC *Hidden*, *secret*, enigmatic.

CRYPTOGRAM Something written in code or in cipher, i.e., with the meaning *hidden*.

LYEIN *To loosen, to undo*

ANALYZE To resolve a situation into its elements; to take something apart and to examine it minutely.

CATALYST   Literally means completely *loosened* (*cata* = completely). Catalyst is the name given to a substance that causes chemical reactions, but remains unchanged itself.

PARALYZE   To *loosen*; hence, to disable (*para* = at or on the side).

MEGAS   *Big, great*

MEGALOMANIA   Mania for doing *great* or grandiose things.

MEGAPHONE   A device for magnifying sound or directing it toward *greater* volume.

MEGATON   An explosive force equivalent to a million tons of TNT—quite a *big* bang!

MICROS   *Small, tiny*

MICROBE   An extremely *tiny* organism, especially one that produces disease (*bios* = life).

MICROPHONE   An instrument that amplifies a *small*, normal voice so that it can be heard over a large area (*phon* = sound; voice).

MICROSCOPE   An instrument through which one can look at very *tiny* things (*scope* = to look at).

MONOS   *One, alone, solitary*

MONK   Literally means one who lives *alone*; a man who devotes himself to a *solitary*, ascetic life.

MONOGAMY The practice of marrying *one* mate (*gamos* = marriage).

MONOLOGUE A speech made by *one* person (*logue* = speaking).

MONOTHEISM The belief in *one* God (*theism* = belief in God).

MONOTONE *One* unvaried tone of voice. Monotonous.

MORPHOS *Shape, form*

The Greek god of sleep was named Morpheus because he shaped the dreams that appeared during sleep. Related to Morpheus is MORPHINE, a drug that kills pain and causes drowsiness.

ANTHROPOMORPHISM Personification; attributing to something that is not human the *form* or other characteristics of man (*anthropos* = man).

METAMORPHOSIS A change in *form*; a complete transformation.

AMORPHOUS Without definitive *shape* or *form*; *formless*.

NAUTICOS
Pertaining to ships and sailing on the sea

ASTRONAUT One who travels in outer space. The word literally means one who *sails* to the stars (*aster* = star), but this is, of course, an exaggeration; the nearest star is trillions of miles away from Earth.

NAUSEA *Seasickness*; queasiness.

NAVIGATE   Originally meant to travel by *ship*. Now, NAVI-
GATE also means to direct an airplane.

POLIS *City or state*

METROPOLIS   A very large *city*. A METROPOLIS is, as it
were, the mother *city* (*metro* = mother).

POLICE   Those who maintain public order in the *city*.

POLITICS   The art of running the *city* or *state*.

POLICY   A course of action thought to be good and expe-
dient, particularly in governing a *city* or *state*. (The
word POLICY meaning an insurance policy is different,
deriving from the French *police*. Originally a certifi-
cate, POLICY came to mean a contract from the sixteenth century onward.)

POLY *Many*

POLYCHROME   *Many*-colored.

POLYGAMY   Marriage to several mates (*gamy* = marriage).

POLYGON   A *many*-angled figure (*gon* = angle).

POLYTHEISM   Belief in *many* gods (*theism* = belief in
God).

PYR *Fire*

PYRE   A funeral *fire*.

PYREX   A type of glass that is resistant to *fire*.

PYROMANIA   A serious mental disorder in which the victim has an uncontrollable urge to set *fires*.

PYROTECHNICS   The scientific word for the much more popular expression *fireworks*.

THERMOS   *Heat*

FURNACE   Oven or similar apparatus that produces *heat*. How do we go from the Greek *therm* to FURNACE? Pronounce the sounds *th* and *f*. The areas of the mouth used to make these sounds are very close to each other. Because of this proximity, *th* and *f* are often interchanged; for example, the name *Theodore* is *Feodor* in Russian. Likewise, the Greek *therm* became *forma* in Latin, and thus provided the root of FURNACE.

THERMOMETER   An instrument that measures *heat* (*meter* = measure).

THERMOS   A bottle that retains the *heat* of liquids.

THERMOSTAT   An instrument for regulating temperature. Basically, a THERMOSTAT works by causing the *heat* to stand (*stat* = stand). In other words, the THERMOSTAT prevents the heat from rising after a certain desired point has been reached.

ZOION   *Animal or living thing*

PROTOZOA   Microscopic form of *animal life*. PROTOZOA

are among the first and most ancient forms of life (*proto* = first).

ZOO   A place where *animals* live in captivity.

ZOOLOGY   The study of *animals* (*ology* = the study of).

Quiz 16

ARE YOU A GOOD WORD DETECTIVE?

Fill in the blanks with the proper Greek-derived English word.

1. The Greek prefix *a* or *an* means WITHOUT. *Gno* is TO KNOW. When the philosopher T.H. Huxley wanted to coin an English word meaning a man who was not sure whether or not God existed, he took these two Greek word elements, *a* (not), and *gno* (to know), and created the word _____.

2. *Arch* is TO RULE. A word implying a state of affairs in which there is no rule, no law, and no order is _____.

3. *Homo* is a Greek word meaning THE SAME. When milk is mixed by machine so thoroughly that you can no longer

distinguish between the cream and the milk, we say that the milk has been (the root *gen* = to make) _____.

4. The ancients believed that the earth was round. The Greek philosopher Plato called the lands that were at the other end of the world (*anti* = against; *ped* = foot) the _____.

5. *Mono* means ONE and *arch* is TO RULE. A person who is the sole ruler is called a _____.

6. *Aster* is a STAR and *dis* is BAD. If you've had some very bad luck or you've come under the influence of a bad star, you're suffering a _____.

7. *Gamo* is a Greek word meaning a WEDDING, a very popular institution. A word meaning "to marry many times" (*poly* = many) is _____. Sticking to one spouse is _____. A man who marries two women (*bi* = two) commits _____.

8. *Helio* is SUN, and the very important idea, first enunciated by Copernicus, that the sun is the center of our planetary system, is called _____.

Answers on page 182

English Borrows Words from the Semitic Languages

English has borrowed words from other Indo-European languages besides the trio of French, Latin, and Greek. It has also borrowed from other language families, among them, the Semitic languages.

The Semitic group is a great family of languages, including Arabic, Hebrew, Aramaic, and Ethiopic. The Semitic and the Indo-European families have lived in proximity for thousands of years, and the two language families have borrowed freely from each other.

Words of Arabic Origin

Many English words that come from Arabic begin with the syllable *al*, which is the definite article "the" in Arabic. For example, ALCOHOL, ALBATROSS, ALCHEMY, ALFALFA, and ALKALI are all of Arabic origin.

ALGEBRA   A branch of mathematics. That this word is of Arabic origin speaks of the Arab preeminence in the field of mathematics during the Middle Ages.

ASSASSIN   Murderer. This word actually comes from the narcotic drug called *hashish* in Arabic. In the early Middle Ages, a secret order of Muslims were swore to murder all Crusaders. They committed their murderous acts, while under the influence of hashish. Thus, strictly speaking, they were the first ASSASSINS.

CHECKMATE   In chess, to CHECKMATE is to capture the opponent's king, and thereby win the game. CHECKMATE is a combination of two Persian words: *shāh* (king) and *mat* (dead). But *māt* (dead) is a word borrowed from Arabic. It literally means the king is dead.

MAGAZINE   From the word *makhzan* (storehouse), MAGAZINE means a place where goods or supplies are stored. Today, we usually use this sense of the word in reference to a warehouse for ammunition. A synonym for magazine is ARSENAL, and it, too, is of Arabic origin.

The more common meaning of MAGAZINE is a periodical that usually contains a miscellaneous collection of articles, stories, poems, pictures, etc. In this sense, too, it is a storehouse—of literature rather than ammunition.

ZERO   Comes from the word *sifr* (empty), cipher. ZERO is the numerical symbol "0," which denotes the absence of quantity. The Arabic concept of ZERO was a vital contribution to our present numerical system. The superiority of Arabic numerals over Roman numerals compares to the superiority of the alphabet over the ancient hieroglyphics.

Words Borrowed from Hebrew

ALPHABET   This familiar English word comes from the first two letters of the Hebrew alphabet—*aleph* and *bet.*

AMEN   There are perhaps a billion words in the world's three or four thousand languages, but there is only one word that has entered 1,200 different languages—the Hebrew word AMEN.

In 250 B.C., the Egyptian king Ptolemy Philadelphus desired a translation of the Hebrew Bible into Greek, the language he understood. According to the traditional account, seventy-two Hebrew scholars worked on the translation—the first written translation ever made from one language to another.

At first, whenever the scholars came to the word AMEN, they wrote out in Greek its exact meaning: "May this prayer come true." But the translation began to get cluttered with the many repetitions of this whole sentence. To remedy the situation, one of the translators suggested introducing the Hebrew word AMEN into the Greek language.

This was only the beginning. In the year 400, St. Jerome translated the Hebrew Bible into Latin. He followed the earlier example, and introduced AMEN into Latin. The Bible has now been translated into 1,200 different languages. The translators of the Bible have always carried over the word AMEN into their translations.

BABBLE   From the Biblical story of the Tower of *Babel* comes BABBLE, to utter meaningless sounds. It is this same story, of course, that accounts for the multitude of tongues spoken throughout the world.

JOT   The tiniest letter in the ancient Hebrew alphabet was *yod*. Its minute size always impressed those who learned to write. In Latin, this letter was pronounced *jot*, and in Greek, it became *iota*.

As an English noun, JOT means a tiny, little bit. As a verb, it is to write briefly, noting only the essential details.

JUBILEE   This word originates from *yōbhēl*, meaning ram's horn, or trumpet. Every fifty years, ancient Hebrew law required a general release of all slaves and a return of all lands to their original owners. These were naturally years of great rejoicing and celebration. The blowing of the ram's horn signified the onset of the *jubilee*.

JUBILEE is used in English to mean a notable anniversary. Strictly speaking, it should be used only for a fiftieth anniversary, but, as often happens, the meaning has been expanded. Related to JUBILEE are JUBILATION (joy) and JUBILANT (expressing exultation).

TO RAISE CAIN   This expression comes from the Biblical story of *Cain* and Abel. Its meaning—to create a disturbance or uproar—is somewhat of an understatement, considering the havoc created by *Cain* as the first murderer.

SACK   The Hebrew word *sāq* corresponds to the Latin *saccus* and the Greek *sakkos*; they all mean bag or sack. As a verb, SACK means to plunder; presumably, looters carried their booty off in *sacks*. There are other forms of this word in English, for example:

SACHET   A small bag or packet, usually containing perfumed powder.

SATCHEL   A small bag, usually of leather or canvas.

Quiz 17

ARE YOU A GOOD WORD DETECTIVE?

Fill in the blanks with the proper Hebrew-derived English word.

1. Oddly enough, the word *jockey*, the *jack* in words like *steeplejack* and *lumberjack*, the mechanical device called a *jack*, all go back to the same Biblical Hebrew name _____, the favored son of Abraham.

2. The Hebrew *sh* usually becomes an *s* in English, so Hebrew *shabbat* became SABBATH; the Hebrew tree named *shigma* became SYCAMORE. The English word _____, a deep bow accompanied by a cry of greeting, comes from the Hebrew word *shalom.*

3. A *sabbatical* is a leave or vacation that occurs every _____ years, because the *Sabbath* comes every _____ days.

Answers on page 182

Word Stories

In the course of sleuthing, a word detective accumulates word stories—interesting facts and anecdotes that deal with the origin of words or phrases.

These tales provide just a glimpse of the fascinating story of words. They show how tricks of history, along with social customs and prejudices, affect our language; how seemingly disparate words may in fact derive from a common origin; how linguistic errors can produce startling results.

Michelangelo's Statue of Moses

St. Peter's Church in Rome has a beautiful statue of Moses, sculpted by Michelangelo in the sixteenth century. Two horns rise from Moses' head. This oddity prompts a question: why did the great artist portray Moses in this strange way?

The answer can be found in what was perhaps the greatest single linguistic error in all history. Let us see what happened.

In Hebrew, the root word *keren* means a HORN. Some ancient Hebrew, looking at the rays of the setting sun, poetically described them as the HORNS of the sun. Thus, the word *keren* also came to mean "a ray of light."

The Bible says that when Moses came down from Mt.

Sinai carrying the Ten Commandments, "the skin of his face shone." The Hebrew word that means SHONE in this passage is *karan*, from the ray of light described by the root *keren*. the root *keren*.

When St. Jerome translated the Hebrew Bible into Latin, in the fifth century, he mistranslated this verse, writing "horns formed on Moses' head." St. Jerome had mistaken the original meaning of *keren*—horn—for its actual usage in the Bible—shone.

A thousand years later, this error had not been corrected. Before creating the sculpture of Moses, Michelangelo went to the Vulgate of St. Jerome to read the story he wished to depict. The artist, in turn, translated St. Jerome's error into his sculpture, portraying Moses with two horns coming from his forehead.

Anglo-Saxon vs. French

In Britain, during the Middle Ages, animals were largely cared for by Anglo-Saxon peasants. As long as the animals were alive, they were fed and herded and named by the Anglo-Saxons. But when the animals were slaughtered and prepared as food, the Norman-French conquerors took over. They, as the wealthy, ruling class, had the privilege of eating meat. Thus, we have an interesting series of contrasting words:

Anglo-Saxon Origin	*Norman-French Origin*
pig	pork
cow	beef
sheep, lamb	mutton
calf	veal
deer	venison

Right and Left; Right and Wrong

The prejudices of the right-handed majority of the world's population are reflected in our speech. The right hand is of course, the *right* one to use. *Dexter* is Latin for RIGHT hand; the word DEXTEROUS means "skillful; clever." The word RIGHT in French is *droit*; from it, we have ADROIT (skillful).

On the other hand, the words that indicate LEFT are rather uncomplimentary. The Latin word for LEFT hand is *sinister*, which in English means "evil; ominous." In French, the word is *gauche*; GAUCHE in English means "clumsy; boorish."

To Cancel and a Chancellor

Cancelli is Latin for CROSSBARS, or lattice. CROSSBARS used to be familiar in ticket windows, separating the customer from the ticket seller. Latticework was ideal for separating an official and those who came to see him, because they could still converse and see each other. However, the lattice was a barrier that maintained a respectable distance between a figure of authority and those beneath him.

The word *cancelli* came to be used in two fantastically different ways:

In the Middle Ages, parchment was extremely expensive. If a monk or scribe made a mistake in copying, he would not scratch out the error, lest he damage the costly vellum. Instead, a standard way of indicating an error developed: the scribe would draw a series of crisscross lines over the mistake. These crisscross lines looked exactly like the crossbars of the latticework. And so, as you can probably guess, the act of crossing out an error came to be called CANCELLING, from the Latin word for lattice, *cancelli*.

In time, the hard *c* of CANCEL began to soften, eventually becoming a *ch* sound—CHANCEL. The official who sat at the chancel was called a CHANCELLOR, and he could be found in courts, in churches, in offices.

Many centuries ago, the CHANCELLOR was really a minor official, having about the same status as a clerk today. But in time, the power and dignity of the office of the CHANCELLOR rose, and the word began to be applied to higher and higher official ranks. Today, the word usually refers to the head of a great university or to the head of a department of government.

The Men on Horseback

A sharp distinction was always made between those who traveled on foot and those who rode horseback. Generally speaking, the men on horseback were rich, powerful, and proud. They looked down scornfully at those who had to walk; and their contempt has come down to us through language.

The word PEDESTRIAN, as a noun, means "one who walks." As an adjective, it means "prosaic, dull, lacking imagination." In chess, the piece that has the smallest value is the pawn, or the foot soldier.

On the other hand, the word CHIVALRY, which derives from the French word for horseman, *chevalier*, refers to exalted or distinguished company. CHIVALROUS means "knightly, valorous, courteous." The adjective CAVALIER, however, means "arrogant, supercilious"—a bit of social commentary of which the PEDESTRIAN would no doubt approve!

Do people who drive automobiles today have the same general contempt for PEDESTRIANS? Is that why there are so many accidents?

So Long Really Means Hello

Did you know that whenever you say "so long," you are really saying HELLO?

Although this sounds silly, it happens to be literally true, as we shall soon see.

What does the word HELLO mean? You probably never stopped to think about it, but all greeting and farewell words have direct meanings. For example, GOODBYE is a shortened way of saying *God be with you*. FAREWELL means *May things fare well with you*. ADIEU is actually a wish that *God be with you*, and AU REVOIR signifies *I hope to see you again*.

HELLO is a form of the more poetic, more ancient greeting word "hail," which in turn is a form of the word "hale." *Hale* means sound or healthy. We speak of a person being *hale* and *hearty*. *Hale* is another form of the word "whole," which is a form of the word "heal." In a sense, when a doctor *heals* you, he is making you a *whole* person again.

Thus, whenever you lift a telephone receiver and say HELLO, you are really saying "I hope that you are whole"—that no part of the person you speak to is missing or broken or bruised. HELLO really means something special.

Now let's look at SO LONG.

Perhaps you have heard of the Hebrew greeting *shalom*. The word has come to mean "peace," but actually the root *shalom* means "whole; all in one piece." Thus, like HELLO, the greeting means "I hope that you are whole and that no part of you is missing or broken or bruised." In Arabic, a sister language of Hebrew, the word is pronounced *salaam*.

In the early twentieth century, the English maintained a large military establishment on the Malay Peninsula. The Malayans were Moslems; Arabic was a sacred language to them. They used the word *salaam* daily as their usual word of greeting. But they pronounced *salaam* through the nose, so that it sounded something like *salang*.

The British soldiers liked the sound of *salang*, and they began to use it themselves. Even when they retired from military service and returned to Britain, many soldiers continued using the word. In time, their neighbors, too, adopted the word, and it was often heard in conversation.

But something interesting happened. *Salang* is just a nonsense word in English. It has no literal meaning whatsoever. English-speaking people, in order to make some sense out of this nonsense word, made two slight changes: they changed *sa* to *so* and *lang* to *long*.

The resulting combination is also nonsense. It has no real meaning as a farewell word. Literally, of course, it means very long! But "so" is a word and "long" is a word and, for this reason, it seems to make more sense than uttering *salang*.

Let us retrace our steps.

So LONG derives from the Arabic *salaam* and from the Hebrew *shalom*. It means "I hope that you are whole."

HELLO also means "I hope that you are whole." So whenever you say "so long," you are really saying "hello."

Parasol and Umbrella

Actually, a PARASOL and an UMBRELLA have the same basic meaning and function.

PARASOL consists of the Latinate word elements *para* (for) and *sol*, (sun). A PARASOL provides protection against the heat of the sun.

Umbra means "shade" in Latin. Originally, an UMBRELLA created shade to protect one from the heat of the sun—just as a PARASOL does. Today, of course, we use UMBRELLAS as protection against the rain, which, in our temperate climate, is more common than intense heat.

An Ounce Is an Inch

In the twelfth century, the city of Troyes, France, was famous for its annual commercial fairs. Merchants from all parts of Europe came to Troyes with their wares. To keep business flowing smoothly, they needed a standard set of weights and measures.

The unit of weight adopted was the pound, consisting of twelve ounces. The twelve-ounce pound, still used today by jewelers and druggists, is known as "troy weight."
The more familiar sixteen-ounce pound was developed later, to accommodate bulkier but cheaper goods, such as potatoes and coal.

In Latin, *uncia* means one-twelfth. The word OUNCE derived from *uncia*, and originally referred to one-twelfth of the pound originating in Troyes. As often happened, the hard *c* in the Latin *uncia* softened to *ch*, yielding the English word INCH, or one-twelfth of a foot.

Thus, in a manner of speaking, the word OUNCE is the same as the word INCH.

We have now come to the end of the road. We hope that you have enjoyed the long journey, and that the work has not been too exhausting for you—intellectually speaking.

We hope that your word-detective skills have grown, and that you now look at words with a respect and admiration that you perhaps did not have before.

If some sense of the wonder of words has been communicated to you by *Word Detective*, we will feel very happy indeed!

Answers to Quizzes

Quiz 1 . . . . **page 29**

1. Break, fast
2. Nonsense
3. Nabbed
4. Shepherd
5. Ship
6. Way
7. Well

Quiz 2 . . . . **page 33**

1. Fib
2. Fourteen
3. Not ever
4. Pestilence
5. Electricity
6. Influenza
7. Revolver

Quiz 3 . . . . **page 37**

1. Rumbling
2. Chugged
3. Cawing
4. Shrieked, squealed squealing, oinking
5. Shriek, cry
6. Snap, crackle, pop
7. Roared, zoomed

Quiz 4 . . . . **page 44**

1. Egypt
2. Cereal
3. Music
4. Museum
5. India
6. India
7. Sweden
8. Cinderella
9. Volcano

Quiz 5 . . . . **page 50**

1. Curriculum
2. Pastor
3. Air
4. Curfew
5. Bitten
6. Brass
7. Bounds
8. Route
9. Accounting
10. Infraction

Quiz 6 . . . . **page 57**

1. Pattern
2. Rolling
3. Rags

4. Endorse
5. Flatterer
6. Role
7. Explain
8. Line
9. Prove
10. Windfall
11. Insane
12. Rules
13. Passed
14. Extradition

Quiz 7 . . . . page 70

1. Hostel
2. Marshal
3. Genes
4. Flex
5. Balm
6. Knave
7. Boulder
8. Brayed
9. Serial

Quiz 8 . . . . page 78

1. Bank
2. Banquet
3. Chariot
4. Pitcher
5. Arcade
6. Archer
7. Commander

Quiz 9 . . . . page 84

1. Super
2. Illiterate
3. Irrigation
4. Misery
5. Contra, against
6. Pass
7. Eloping
8. Interloper
9. Supreme

Quiz 10 . . . . page 105

1. Antidote
2. Prejudice
3. Despair
4. Rules
5. Inclement
6. Fail
7. Retailers
8. Disguising
9. Discount, *dis*
10. Diameter
11. Veil
12. Automobile
13. Ease

Quiz 11 . . . . page 110

1. Spinsters, youngster,
   gangster
2. Miserable
3. Awe
4. Plumber

5. Line
6. Quarrel
7. Slow
8. Lock
9. Broad
10. Found, darling,
    yearling

Quiz 12 .... page 114

1. Floats   8. Tumbled
2. Vacation   9. Ducked
3. Lug   10. Count
4. Appears
5. Noses
6. Image
7. Jammed

Quiz 13 .... page 120

1. Ghost
2. Fancy
3. Palm
4. Morphine
5. Mystery
6. Inferno
7. Dismal
8. Doom
9. Clairvoyance

Quiz 14 .... page 139

1. Patients
2. Candle

3. Albino
4. Verdict
5. Illustrations
6. Style
7. Library

Quiz 15 .... page 151

1. Butler
2. Insurance
3. Parlor
4. Court
5. Disease
6. Rendezvous

Quiz 16 .... page 165

1. Agnostic
2. Anarchy
3. Homogenized
4. Antipodes
5. Monarch
6. Disaster
7. Polygamy, monogamy,
   bigamy
8. Heliocentrism

Quiz 17 .... page 171

1. Jacob
2. Salaam
3. Seven, seven

Hart Publishing Company, Inc.
New York City